EST MARATHON '96
The One-Act Plays

SMITH AND KRAUS PUBLISHERS
Contemporary Playwrights / Collections

EST MARATHON '96
The One-Act Plays

CONTEMPORARY PLAYWRIGHTS
SERIES

SK
A Smith and Kraus Book

A Smith and Kraus Book
Published by Smith and Kraus, Inc.
PO Box 127, Lyme, NH 03768

First Edition: June 1998
10 9 8 7 6 5 4 3 2 1

The Library of Congress Cataloging-In-Publication Data
EST Marathon '96: the one-act plays / edited by Marisa Smith. —1st ed.
    p.   cm.   —(Contemporary playwrights series) ISSN 1067-9510
    ISBN 1-57525-135-3

    1. One-act plays, American. 2. American drama—20th century. 3. Ensemble Studio Theater.
I. Smith, Marisa. II. Series.

    PS627.053E88   1995
    812'.04108—dc20

                          95-2287
                           CIP

CONTENTS

English
(It's Where the Words Are)

BY PETER BASCH

TO
CURT DEMPSTER AND STEVE KAPLAN.

THE AUTHOR

Peter Basch is a native Manhattanite who attended the Lycée Français de New-York and Columbia College, where he graduated with a degree in Physics. He briefly attended graduate school at U.C. Berkeley, but was so distracted by the Drama Department, where he played Sir Amorous LaFoole in Ben Jonson's *Epicoene,* that he dropped out eight months later. Peter returned to New York where he appeared as Polixenes in *Winters Tale* and Count Rostòv in *War and Peace.* He then worked for two years as a French-English tour guide at the United Nations, from which he still retains a very handsome necktie.

In 1984 Peter joined the Manhattan Punch Line Comedy Corps, and played KJ in Mike Eisenberg's *Hackers.* His association with the Punch Line continued until its demise in 1991. During his tenure in the Comedy Corps, and later as an Artist in Residence, Peter did readings of hundreds of new plays and appeared in the Punch Line One Act Festivals. He created roles in David Ives' *7 Menus,* Howard Korder's *Wonderful Party* and Laurence Klavan's *Uncle Lumpy Comes to Visit.* As part of the Punch Lines's sketch comedy group, *Another Fine Mess,* Peter started writing and directing.

Peter's association with the Ensemble Studio Theater began in 1990 when he attended Curt Dempster's Theatre Lab at their annual Summer Conference. In 1993 and 1994 he was the Conference's Literary Manager, running the weekend reading series. In May 1993, Peter became a member of the Ensemble. In the Summer Conference of 1992, Peter wrote the ten-minute play *Primates,* which spawned his full-length, *The Coven,* which was a finalist in the HBO New Writers Project in 1994. But it took his short play *English (It's Where the Words Are)* to win a spot in the 1995 (second and last) New Writers Project.

English (etc.) then went on to garner a spot in EST's 1996 Marathon of One-Acts where it was received with a rave by the *New York Times.* It then made it to the U.S. Comedy Arts Festival in Aspen, sponsored by HBO, where it won the MCI Jury Award (the only award offered in the festival). It was then featured in the Bumbershoot Festival in Seattle, where it received excellent notices in the *Seattle Times.*

Peter's original animation, *Naked Mole Rats,* has been optioned by Klasky/Csupo and is in the process of being developed.

ORIGINAL PRODUCTION

English: It's Where the Words Are was originally produced at the HBO New Writers Project in October 1995 with the following cast:

Joey . . . . Justin Louis
Suzy . . . . Rhonda Hayter

It was subsequently produced at the 1996 Ensemble Studio Theatre Marathon with the following cast:

Joey . . . . Joseph Lyle Tayler
Suzy . . . . Stephanie Cannon

AUTHOR'S NOTE

In 1995 I was a reader for the EST Marathon. We each had to write coverages on one hundred plays. At least sixty of mine were about angst-ridden, barely articulate blue-collar types groping for words to express their volcanic (namely 'primitive') emotions. When they inevitably fail, they either resort to violence or they blossom forth with spontaneous blue-collar poetry. Or both. This thuddingly tedious stereotype is at least as old as Jean-Jaques Rousseau's Noble Savage. Not only that, but (trust me on this) these plays were mostly written by well-educated middle- to upper-class types (which I am too, by the way) who simultaneously romanticize and patronize people who work with their hands. The stereotype may have originated with Rousseau, but its modern avatar was perfected in the Group Theatre and the Actors' Studio, where "inarticulate" was equated with "authentic." Marlon Brando's muscular "mumbler" persona originated under the bookish, articulate Lee Strasberg. So here is my take on this stereotype, with nods to *The Honeymooners* and *Playhouse 90*.

CHARACTERS

JOEY
SUZY

PLACE

A run-down tenement.

TIME

Since the 30s.

Joey, a maleducated dreamer, is sitting on the window sill. Suzy is in the kitchen. On the counter is a short pyramid of #10 cans of Dinty Moore beef stew.

SUZY: Whatcha lookin' at alla time, Joey? Huh? Whatcha lookin' at alla time?

JOEY: Nuffin.

SUZY: Cmon, Joey, whatcha lookin at?

JOEY: Nuffin.

SUZY: You're always lookin out that window, Joey, what's out there, huh, what's out there that we don't have in here, huh, Joey, whatcha lookin at?

JOEY: Nuffin.

SUZY: Tell me…*(Beat.)* huh, Joey…*(Beat.)* huh, Joey…*(Two beats.)* huh, Joey, whatcha lookin at? Don't tell me it's nuffin, Joey.

JOEY: Nuff…uh, nuffin.

SUZY: Dontcha love me no more, Joey? Whatcha keep lookin at?

JOEY: Yeah, yeah, I love ya.

SUZY: Dontcha love me no more, Joey?

JOEY: Yeah, I love ya.

SUZY: Dontcha love me?

JOEY: Yeah, I love ya.

SUZY: Look in here!

JOEY: *(Looks at her.)* Huh?

SUZY: Nuffin.

(Joey looks out the window.)

SUZY: I try to make a nice home for ya, Joey. So ya won't have ta look out no windows. So everything you could want would be inside. I made a nice Dinty Moore for ya, Joey, just like ya like. So ya won't have ta look outta no windows. I hate windows. Why d'ya look outta them?

JOEY: Don' know, Suzy.

SUZY: Why d'ya look outta them?

JOEY: Don't know, Suzy.

SUZY: Huh, why, Joey?

(Joey turns to face her.)

JOEY: I'll tell ya why, Suzy, 'cause I feel like a little part of me, not like a body part, like a kidney, but a part that's inside a me anyway, even though, strictly speaking, it's not a body part, this part, see, is gettin real small. I can barely express it because I am so maleducated, but it's a part a me, an' it's small. An' I feel like…when I look out, this part a me gets bigger an' bigger…

SUZY: Expands.

JOEY: Yeah, like *expands* ta fill alla space. An' it makes me feel like…I'm not just the guy wiping up the spilled gasoline at the station, but like I'm like a bird, not like a pigeon, but like one a them birds I saw at the zoo when I was little, one of the birds at that place where they have the birds…

SUZY: Aviary.

JOEY: Yeah, the *aviary*, the ones wit' the, you know, all the feathers like, the ones wit' the…

SUZY: Plumage.

JOEY: Yeah, the *plumage* all over the place, the ones that fly so high, so high, that the sun himself is jealous of how high the bird wit' the *plumage* in the *aviary* can fly. I wanna feel like that. Not like some lowly…

SUZY: Slug.

JOEY: Yeah, some lowly *slug* in the dirty, the dirty…

SUZY: Putrescence.

JOEY: Yeah, some lowly *slug* crawling through the dirty *putrescence*. Ya know?

SUZY: Have some Dinty Moore. You'll feel better.

JOEY: *(Comes to the table.)* I dunno, Suzy. I just don't know. Sometimes I think an' I think an' I still don't know.

SUZY: I know.

JOEY: Ya know?

SUZY: I know.

JOEY: Ya know?

SUZY: I know. Jus' eat, Joey.

(Joey reluctantly sits to eat. He lowers his head and eats like the dedicated trencherman he is, noisily and with gusto. Suzy plays abstractedly with her food.)

SUZY: I jus' feel…I feel like…it's just that I feel like…I just feel like…

(Joey, chewing, looks up at Suzy.)

SUZY: I feel like I hate that window, Joey, because I want this home to be the only place for you, I want you to be so happy here that you brick the window up, and weld the door shut with that oxy-acetylene torch of yours and hold me, Joey, and just hold me, Joey, and just hold me, Joey, and crush me wit' your arms, Joey, crush me an' I'll crush you until all our body parts get all mixed up together, just like this stew…

(Joey stops chewing, looks down at his stew.)

SUZY: …and then the little crushed parts of our bodies reach to each other like little blind slugs, they, like, extend cilia an' tendrils an' stuff an' pull at each other an' rejoin each other an' reconnect an' link up an' become like a new being, a better being, a being made a the best parts of both of us, the finer, better, finer, better, parts, an' never have to leave each other again.

(Beat. Joey starts eating again.)

SUZY: Ya know what I mean?

JOEY: Hng?

SUZY: Ya know? Ya know what I mean? Ya know?

JOEY: Hng.

SUZY: You know.

JOEY: Hng.

SUZY: There's just one thing, Joey.

JOEY: Hng?

SUZY: Just one thing. The stakes…

JOEY: *(Perking up considerably, his mouth full.)* Steaks?

SUZY: Yeah. They're not high enough.

JOEY: *(Confused.)* Hng?

SUZY: We're just sort of talking aimlessly, repeating ourselves like cretins. We need higher stakes. We need…a firearm.

(Suzy somehow produces an impossibly huge silver gun. Joey does a spit take all over the table.)

JOEY: PTOOOEY!

SUZY: I'll kill you, Joey, I swear I will, unless you, unless you…

JOEY: What?

SUZY: Unless you…

JOEY: What? What?

SUZY: Unless you…

JOEY: What do you want me to do? What? I'll do anything!

SUZY: I know. The gun was a cheap tactic.

(Joey backs down and considers gun warily.)

SUZY: *(Bittersweet, toying with gun.)* I remember old Monsignor Vitelli, how whenever little Santos pulled a gun he would smile that crooked little smile a his an' take off those silver little half-glasses a his an' wipe 'em with that little lace hanky a his 'til they shone like little twin stars; an' shakin' his head in that little disappointed way he had he'd put his little half glasses a his back on, but he was shakin' his head so he'd poke himself in the eye with the earpiece of his glasses, an' how that day a his, he poked the earpiece into his eye an' kept shakin' his head in his disappointed way, so the eyeball got levered out by the earpiece of his glasses, an' it bounced on his desk an' bounced on the floor an' rolled under the credenza; an' how he laughed that little squeaky laugh a his, an' how we all got on our knees an' looked under the credenza, an' how Santos got down there with a flashlight an' a broom handle an' looked but it was gone. It had gone to that far, deep, dark, place where stuff goes that rolls under dressers an' credenzas, the cufflinks an' the earrings an' the eyeballs an' the comic books an' the feather boas an' the innocence a childhood an', an', an'...Oh, Joey. An' only when they tore the building down an' ripped up the foundation, a subcontractor named Stavros found the eyeball in the electrical system an' kept it as a charm on his keychain.

JOEY: You wanna put the gun away?

SUZY: Huh?

JOEY: The gun. You're scaring me.

SUZY: Weren't you moved by my speech?

JOEY: Speech?

SUZY: Yeah. My revealing personal reminiscence opening up my deepest personal soul and so on.

JOEY: To tell the honest unvarnished truth I kind of stopped listening when you pulled the gun.

SUZY: You missed the whole thing?

JOEY: Firearms do that to me. I get kind of a buzz in my ears. Can't hear too good.

SUZY: Too well.

JOEY: Too well.

(Suzy puts gun away.)

SUZY: I'm leaving you Joey.

JOEY: Why?

SUZY: Because you don't listen to me. That's why.

JOEY: Well, did you have to pull a gun on me?

SUZY: I only did that to make you listen.

JOEY: I woulda listened!

SUZY: No you wouldn't. You're too busy thinking about your own ill-defined yearnings.

JOEY: Well, my ill-defined yearnings are pretty all-consuming.

SUZY: What about my ill-defined yearnings?

JOEY: I didn't know you had any ill-defined yearnings.

SUZY: You think all my yearnings are well-defined?

JOEY: They're not?

SUZY: No! They're as ill-defined as all get-out!

JOEY: What. "Come eat your Dinty Moore" is ill-defined? I'd say it was pretty clear-cut.

SUZY: Well, that's not one of my yearnings. That's just a preference.

JOEY: Oh. What's one of your yearnings?

SUZY: Like...Like...Oh! They're just so ill-defined.

JOEY: Oh, you don't have any.

SUZY: That just shows what you know! You know nothing! You know nothing about me!

JOEY: Whaddaya mean!

SUZY: I'm a complete stranger to you. A puzzle you can't solve, a code you can't break, a cipher you can't decipher, an enigma you can't...uh, make obvious.

JOEY: Whatever the opposite of an enigma is, that's what you are to me.

SUZY: You don't even know my name.

JOEY: Suzy O'Shaughnessy.

SUZY: Okay. You know my name. That was too easy. You don't know my favorite album.

JOEY: Dark Side of the Moon. Pink Floyd.

SUZY: My favorite pizza topping!

JOEY: Sausage and garlic.

SUZY: My blood type!

JOEY: O negative.

SUZY: My dress size!

JOEY: Seven.

SUZY: The time of my birth!

JOEY: Ten forty three AM.

SUZY: My natural hair color!

JOEY: Roan.

SUZY: My allergies!

JOEY: Feathers, ragweed, dust, horses, penicillin.

SUZY: My mother's maiden name!

JOEY: Clary.

SUZY: My father's mother's maiden name!

JOEY: O'Keefe.

SUZY: Their anniversary!

JOEY: Your parents' or your father's parents'.

SUZY: *(Beat.)* My father's parents'.

JOEY: April 6.

SUZY: *(New idea.)* When I lost my virginity.

JOEY: Age seventeen, June 12.

SUZY: Where?

JOEY: Behind the bandshell, among the juniper.

SUZY: With whom?

JOEY: Stinky Hennessy.

SUZY: *(Beat.)* In what position?

JOEY: Wheelbarrow.

SUZY: Did I come?

JOEY: *(Ruefully.)* Yeah.

SUZY: *(Three beats.)* Actually, you know a lot about me.

JOEY: Yeah.

SUZY: *(Beat; now she starts asking things she really wants to know, not just to test him.)* Was I a happy child?

JOEY: Sometimes.

SUZY: Hng. What career should I pursue?

JOEY: Something involving contact with people; teamwork.

SUZY: Is there a true religion?

JOEY: Yes. Hinduism.

SUZY: Really?

JOEY: Yep.

SUZY: Are neutrinos massless?

JOEY: Not completely.

SUZY: *(Beat.)* You're omniscient, aren't you.

JOEY: No.

SUZY: What don't you know?

JOEY: I…I…don't know how to be worthy of your love.

SUZY: Oh, Joey, how can you say that?

JOEY: I am a bum. A bum from a line of bums. You are a queen. Also from a line of bums, admittedly, but still a queen.

SUZY: Oh, Joey, you are no bum.

JOEY: Yes I am.

SUZY: No you're not.

JOEY: I am.

SUZY: You are not.

JOEY: I am.

SUZY: You are not.

JOEY: I am.

SUZY: You are.

JOEY: I am not!

SUZY: See?

JOEY: Why you…

SUZY: Oh, ya big lug. I love ya, even with all your moods.

JOEY: I love you too, Suzy.

    (Fade to heart-shaped gobo.)

THE END

Slice of Life

BY STUART R. BROWN

THE AUTHOR

Stuart R. Brown was born in Perth Amboy, New Jersey, on October 20, 1954. He graduated from Rutgers College in New Brunswick, where he majored in English and earned a Bachelors Degree, and from Brandeis University in Waltham, Massachusetts, studying playwriting in the Theatre Arts Program and earning a Master of Fine Arts Degree. Mr. Brown has taught in the English Departments of Rutgers University, New York University, and New Jersey Institute of Technology. He lives in New York City and Andes, New York, with his wife and daughter.

ORIGINAL PRODUCTION

Slice of Life was originally produced at The Ensemble Studio Theatre May 22–June 2, 1996. It was directed by Pirie MacDonald with the following cast:

Earl . . . . Paul Austin
C.C. . . . . Richmond Hoxie

CHARACTERS

EARL

C.C.

PLACE

Earl's Cafe.

TIME

The present.

The setting is the interior of Earl's Cafe, a modest, diner-type establishment consisting of a counter and five stools, a booth in the corner, and three tables. There is a cash register behind the counter as well as various salt and pepper shakers, condiments and the like. Two glass cover dishes, one for pie and another for cake, are on the counter. The pie dish is empty. One last piece of angel food cake remains. Several dollar bills tacked up on the wall above the cash register. An empty chart, the top of which says "Breakfast Specials," also behind counter. A door, up right: the entrance. Another door, down left: a storeroom for supplies and a rest room. The one window, up center, looks out on a bleak, wintry landscape with snow on the windowsill, icicles hanging down from above it, and the wan light of mid-morning coming through. When the lights come up, Earl is behind the counter, wiping it down with a damp cloth. C.C. enters. He is wearing a long overcoat, gloves and a stocking cap. Earl looks up at him; C.C. looks at Earl. The latter continues to the door, down left; opens it and exits, closing it behind him. Earl resumes wiping down the counter, more vigorously. After a moment C.C. comes out of the rest room and proceeds to the counter where he stands uncertainly next to one of the stools.

EARL: Aren't you going to sit down?

C.C.: Oh, yeah. *(Sits on a stool.)*

EARL: Cold out, isn't it?

C.C.: Yeah.

EARL: My driveway was a sheet of ice when I went out this morning. I could've killed myself coming in here. I could have. And you should've seen my street. All ice and snow. Snow banked up on the sidewalk, six, seven foot high. Six day old snow. From the last snowstorm. The one last week. It's pretty damn bad is all I can tell you. And no sign of a warm trend. Not one in sight. How do you like that? Hey, 'you all right? You look like your cat died.

C.C.: My cat did die.

EARL: Are you kidding? You're kidding, right? You're not kidding. You're not kidding, are you?

C.C.: No. I'm not kidding.

EARL: Well, what was 'e matter with 'im, if you don't mind me asking?

C.C.: He was real sick. He could hardly walk. His hind legs were paralyzed, first the right one and then the left. He fell a couple of times and hit his head. I had to carry him to his food bowls. Or bring the bowls over to where he was. He rarely moved from in front of the radiator. He made a place for himself on the rug in front of the radiator and he rarely moved from it.

EARL: Well, I'm really sorry to hear that. Would you like something to eat? Cup of coffee, maybe.

C.C.: No. I'm not very hungry. He had blood in his stool. It was very watery. The vet didn't know what was wrong with him. He did all these tests but he didn't know what it was.

EARL: Sometimes they don't know.

C.C.: Yeah. This was one of those times.

EARL: Those are the breaks.

C.C.: Some breaks.

EARL: Take the good with the bad.

C.C.: Good with the bad.

EARL: There's always going to be bad, along with the good. Look at me. I had to shut this place down already two times because of bad weather and it isn't even February yet. 'You see me complaining? No. I grin and bear it. Chin up, I say to myself. Keep going. Grin and bear it. I risk my life every morning coming in here. Some mornings, there aren't even any customers. If I slip on the ice, I'm a goner. I haven't got a prayer. If I break my arm or my hip I'll have to call it quits. You won't see me slinging hash or flipping burgers with my arm in a cast or my leg in some brace. Who's going to run the place? I'd have to close it down. Are you sure you don't want something to eat? It might make you feel better if you eat something. How do you like your eggs, over easy or sunny side up?

C.C.: I don't like eggs. I never eat breakfast. And it's too early for lunch. You got any pie?

EARL: No, I don't have any pie. The bakery didn't make a delivery this morning. No pie. I got cake though. I got this piece of cake left.

C.C.: I don't want cake. I feel like pie. 'Felt like a piece of pie.

EARL: Sorry.

C.C.: What kind of cake?

(Earl removes the glass cover; shows C.C. the dish with the piece of cake on it.)

EARL: It's a white cake. Angel food.

C.C.: I like chocolate cake. I'm partial to chocolate cake. If I'm going to eat cake at all it's got to be chocolate.

EARL: Well, I got no chocolate here. It's angel food cake with a coconut cream frosting. It's the last piece.

C.C.: I'll pass.

EARL: Suit yourself. This piece of cake is going to end up in the garbage. I'll never eat it. It'll just sit there.

C.C.: Maybe somebody'll eat it. Somebody ate the rest of it.

EARL: Maybe. Truth be told, a customer sees a piece of cake sitting there, all by itself, you know what they figure? 'You know what conclusion they draw? They surmise that that piece of cake has been sitting there for a long time. Sitting there, uneaten, unwanted. They figure there's something wrong with it. Yeah. I know. I'm in this business thirty-six years. You learn a few tricks. I've seen pieces of cake sit there just like this one like they were contaminated with radioactive isotopes. No customer wants to touch 'em with a ten foot pole. It's pathetic. But it's the truth.

C.C.: I had that cat almost fifteen years.

EARL: What?

C.C.: That's a hundred and five years old in human years. Is it seven years to every one human year with cats, you know, the same way it is with dogs?

EARL: You're asking me?

C.C.: Maybe it's only five. Or is it eight?

EARL: I'm not exactly an animal lover.

C.C.: 'Never had a dog or a cat?

EARL: When I was a kid.

C.C.: You ought to get a dog. Or a cat.

EARL: 'Place is too small. What do I need any pets for? I'm here eleven, twelve hours a day. I'm never home. It would be cruel and unusual punishment for any dog or cat to be placed in that kind of situation. I wouldn't wish it on my worst enemy. What do I want to do that to a poor, defenseless animal for?

C.C.: I don't know. Companionship. Animals are more loyal than people. You can depend on 'em.

EARL: You can depend on people, if it comes down to it.

C.C.: I never could.

EARL: Maybe you haven't met the right people.

C.C.: Maybe I haven't.

EARL: Wait until you meet the right person and then…render an assessment.

C.C.: Yeah. The thing is, I keep expecting to see the cat, and he's not there. Sometimes I think I do see him when I go to make lunch and dinner, when I first wake up in morning. He was always there. Nearly fifteen years of taking care of him, feeding him, changing his litter box, combing out the tangles in his fur. You get used to that.

EARL: Get another one.

C.C.: Another cat?

EARL: Yeah.

C.C.: Naw. I couldn't do that. He wasn't the kind of cat you could replace. I can't do that. Not right away, anyway. It wouldn't be right.

EARL: I had a neighbor who lost his dog. His dog was run over by a delivery van. Right in front of his house. He saw it happen. Cried for days. Grown man crying. You know what he did?

C.C.: What?

EARL: He went right out and got another dog. You see what I'm saying? The guy lost his dog and he got another dog.

C.C.: I couldn't do that.

EARL: Why not?

C.C.: I just couldn't.

EARL: You want to feel sorry for yourself.

C.C.: If I got another cat or even a dog for that matter, it wouldn't change anything. It wouldn't bring my cat back. You don't see people going out and getting another child if their child dies or another father to replace their father if he dies.

EARL: People do it all the time. They get another pet. If their dog dies they go out and get another one. It's the same way with cats. I don't say it's a replacement for the dead pet, but they do it. They do it just the same.

C.C.: Why?

EARL: I don't know. I guess they want something to take care of. 'Keep 'em company. They have their reasons. They have reasons. That's why they do it.

C.C.: I'm not doing it.

EARL: Don't. You're entitled. You're entitled to do it or not do it.

C.C.: I'm not.

EARL: Don't. You're you and they're them. It's your prerogative. Carry a torch for your dead cat. Leave it at that.

C.C.: That's just what I'm going to do.

EARL: If I had a flag I would wave it at half mast. In memory of your cat.

C.C.: Don't—don't make jokes.

EARL: I wasn't joking.

C.C.: What were you doing?

EARL: I don't know. I wasn't joking. I'm sorry. I'm sorry if I offended you.

C.C.: All right...It's all right. It's just...I don't know...nobody understands the gravity of it...

EARL: I'm sorry.

C.C.: …It's no laughing matter.

EARL: No. Maybe he's better off.

C.C.: Better off?

EARL: The cat.

C.C.: Better off? Better off dead?

EARL: Maybe.

C.C.: I don't know how you could think that.

EARL: You know, he was old, you said he was sick, his time had come. Maybe he's better off.

C.C.: 'Be better if he never got old or sick.

EARL: Right. Or if we didn't have to work or pay bills…and there were no taxes. Anything anybody ever wanted came down from above…like rain. And we didn't need any money. Everything was just there. All free. Free for the taking, the asking. Yeah.

C.C.: You think there's a place for cats when they die just like there's supposed to be one for people?

EARL: I never thought about it, but I don't see why not.

C.C.: I guess what I'm really asking is, does a cat have an immortal soul? You know, like people are supposed to have.

EARL: It's more than likely not the same as a human soul. A cat is a different creature to begin with.

C.C.: I like to think that his life doesn't just end with his death.

EARL: You're not wrong in thinking that.

C.C.: I guess nobody really knows until it's time for them to die. Do they?

EARL: I guess some people feel more strongly one way or the other.

C.C.: I guess.

EARL: You ever been married?

C.C.: No. You?

EARL: No.

C.C.: Why'd you ask?

EARL: I don't know. 'Curious, I guess.

C.C.: I lived with somebody once. For a long time, actually. I guess you could say she was like a common law wife.

EARL: How long?

C.C.: Ten years. She used to say she had such high expectations for our relationship. She was always saying that. She said I was a big disappointment to her. I turned out to be a big disappointment.

EARL: What was she expecting? What did she want you to do?

C.C.: Get a better job. Make more money. Be a kinder, gentler sort of person.

That kind of thing. I don't know. I think she didn't want to face the fact that she was tired of the relationship. She was tired of me. That's what it came down to...in the end.

EARL: Were you tired of her?

C.C.: I don't know. I guess I was. I guess I was tired of her too.

EARL: So maybe it's for the best.

C.C.: Maybe. Things never measure up to our expectations. It's one way in our mind and then there's reality. They aren't the same. What's in our mind and what's out there. I guess you could say our expectations are always unrealistic.

EARL: You don't believe in starting over, do you? A clean slate.

C.C.: You mean find another woman. Get another cat. Is that what you mean?

EARL: No. I don't mean that. I don't mean that. No.

C.C.: You ever been in love?

EARL: Everybody's been in love.

C.C.: You really believe that? Everybody's been in love. You believe that?

EARL: I said it, didn't I?

C.C.: That doesn't mean you believe it.

EARL: I said it.

C.C.: Have you ever been in love?

EARL: I just told you what I told you. Didn't I? And you're asking me if I ever been in love. And I just told you what I told you.

C.C.: Tell me the truth.

EARL: No. All right? No. I never been in love. Being in love means somebody's supposed to love you back, right? No. I never been in love. Is that what you wanted to hear?

C.C.: No.

EARL: No?

C.C.: I mean...'Forget it. I'm sorry I brought it up. Just forget it. Can you do that? Can you just forget it?

EARL: No. I can't. It's too late. I can't forget it.

C.C.: Look, I apologized, didn't I? What more do you want?

EARL: I don't want anything. There isn't anything I want.

C.C.: Look, I said I'm sorry. What do you want me to do? If it would make you feel any better, you could serve me that piece of cake.

EARL: Don't do me any favors.

C.C.: No, really I want it. I changed my mind.

EARL: You can't have it. It's not for sale. This piece of cake stays where it is.

C.C.: Does that go for anything else in here? Say I want a cup of coffee or a short stack of flapjacks.

EARL: You out of luck. There's another diner down the road about eleven miles. Maybe he'll serve you.

C.C.: You'd send me out in this weather?

EARL: There's the door.

C.C.: You're refusing a patron of this establishment?

EARL: Since when did you acquire an appetite? You weren't hungry before.

C.C.: I didn't say I wasn't hungry. I wasn't hungry for what you had under that dish.

EARL: And now you want it?

C.C.: Yes. I said I did, didn't I?

EARL: And you did say you weren't hungry. I distinctly heard you say you weren't hungry.

C.C.: Well, I'm hungry now. It doesn't matter whether I was hungry before. I'm hungry now.

EARL: If you're hungry go to a restaurant. You're just hungry now because you want to make it up to me for making me out to be a liar before. I don't need anybody patronizing me that way.

C.C.: Well, if you're not going to serve me any food, I might as well just leave.

EARL: It didn't stop you before.

C.C.: Are you telling me you want me to stay?

EARL: I'm not telling you anything. Just that this cake is not for sale. I don't care whether you stay or go. It's immaterial to me.

C.C.: I can stay and not order anything?

EARL: If you stay I won't serve you anything.

C.C.: I didn't think that was done.

EARL: It's been done…and is being done.

C.C.: Suit yourself. It's your business. I can't make you serve me. If I stayed here and didn't leave you'd have to serve me. If I stayed here eventually you'd have to serve me.

EARL: No I wouldn't.

C.C.: You'd let me starve.

EARL: That's right.

C.C.: Common decency says that after so many days and nights without food in a place where there is food, that the proprietor of that place would make a concession and serve food to a person that needs food, rather than let him starve. Common decency says that.

EARL: Not this proprietor.

C.C.: Who ever said there was any decency in this world?

EARL: I don't know.

C.C.: Who ever said it didn't know what he was talking about. He didn't know what he was talking about when he said it. Well, all right, then. I might as well go. Thanks. Thanks for the conversation. *(Comes off the stool. Starts for the door.)*

EARL: Hey, wait a minute.

(C.C. stops. Earl removes the cover from the cake dish; puts the cake on a plate and places it on the counter. C.C. returns to stool. Earl puts a fork down next to the plate. C.C. eats the cake. Lights fade. Earl pours coffee.)

THE END

Home

BY LAURA CAHILL

THE AUTHOR

Ms. Cahill's play *Hysterical Blindness* has a limited run at the Currican Theatre (New York) and subsequently opened at The Hudson Guild Theatre. Her play *Home* was a part of the EST Marathon '96 and was published by Dramatists Play Service in *3 by EST*. Ms. Cahill's other works include: *The Way* (Naked Angels), *Him and Her* (WBAI-Shelf Life Series), *Last Dance* (EST Octoberfest), and *Stalker* (Naked Angels—Angels in Progress). Her work has been presented at One Dream, Malaparte, West Bank, Westbeth Theatre Center, and First Look L.A.

ORIGINAL PRODUCTION

Home was originally produced at The Ensemble Theatre Studio, June 1996. It was directed by Jace Alexander with the following cast:

Mary Jane . . . . Janet Zarish
Olivia . . . . Helen Gallagher

CHARACTERS

MARY JANE
OLIVIA

The living room of a small suburban development house in New Jersey. It is just after twilight on a Saturday in early summer. The furniture is Colonial reproductions and nothing is expensive. The room is kept immaculately clean. Olivia, 60s, sits on the couch with her cross-stitch. Mary Jane, 40s and very youthful, walks in the front door. She is dressed in worn tight blue jeans and a cheap-looking top. She wears sneakers. This is her exercise ensemble. Her walkman is on and she sings along loudly with the oldie she's listening to as she stretches out from her speed-walk.

MARY JANE: *(Heading to the kitchen.)* I saw two men that I could tell weren't married. One was walkin a dog which I think is pretty good. Men with dogs are more open and friendly, you know?

OLIVIA: Your father always had a dog, from the day I met him he had a dog. I bought Coke. You must be thirsty from all that running.
(Mary Jane emerges from the kitchen with a can of Coke.)

MARY JANE: One fellow looked about forty to forty-five. Which is a good age. The other one was a little older, fifty to fifty-two. *(She walks in and sits with her mother.)* And he was walking just for exercise, which is real good, real good Ma, right? A man who walks for exercise isn't afraid of living. Isn't that right?

OLIVIA: Maybe he's recovering from a bypass.

MARY JANE: I don't know about that.

OLIVIA: They tell you to go out and walk every day after your bypass. That's what Daddy would've been doing right now.

MARY JANE: And Daddy loved living, see? See what I mean? I think I did good.

OLIVIA: But you didn't talk to them?

MARY JANE: No, not on the first day. I gotta let them notice me for awhile. Divorcee back in town, free as a bird, loves to laugh and take long drives.

OLIVIA: Good. There's no big hurry. You could meet a husband anywhere, really.

MARY JANE: I wanna meet him here.
(Pause. Mary Jane waits for a response. Olivia doesn't look up.)

MARY JANE: You know what I did on my way back? I walked down by the railroad tracks.

OLIVIA: Nobody walks down there anymore.

MARY JANE: I used to practically every day. There used to be that candy store, remember? Me and Susie'd sit on the curb in front drinking a Coke. There were those boys who'd come by. Bobby Panko and Tommy

Hansen and Billy Marsh. They'd drive up in their cars...one by one..."You wanna go for a ride, Mary Jane?" God, that was a lifetime ago. I wonder if anybody else remembers that but me.

OLIVIA: People don't think about things like that.

MARY JANE: I don't know. They might.

OLIVIA: People learn to move on.

MARY JANE: What? Are you picking on me already? I didn't come three thousand miles to get picked on.

OLIVIA: Oh, sorry. I didn't realize I was picking on anybody. I thought I was just sitting in my living room minding my own business.

MARY JANE: You'd think you'd be a little happier to hear me talk like this. Here I am coming home after all this time and looking for a nice husband.

OLIVIA: You think you'd be a little more concerned with someone else once in a while—

MARY JANE: I am.

OLIVIA: Like your mother.

MARY JANE: I am concerned.

OLIVIA: I have a lot my mind today.

MARY JANE: I'm concerned with what's on your mind.

(Pause. Olivia waits for Mary Jane. She doesn't respond.)

OLIVIA: Coulda fooled me.

MARY JANE: When I get a husband maybe we'll have the wedding right in this room. I think that's what this house needs now. Huh, Ma?

OLIVIA: We'll have to see.

MARY JANE: It'll be great Everything's gonna work out for me. You'll see. Okay?

OLIVIA: Okay.

MARY JANE: I walked past the St. Cecilia's fairgrounds, you know. Remember how the men would pay to fight with a live bear on that little stage the Monsignor put up every year? I'm sure they don't do that anymore.

OLIVIA: No.

MARY JANE: That would be considered old-fashioned to people now. It's so funny cause I used to think when I was a kid the world had already changed just in time for my childhood—and that everything was modern. But actually it was real old-fashioned when I was a kid. That stuff we all thought about the world then wasn't true at all. And then the world did change and it was without me even noticing it...and it didn't have anything to do with me. My childhood was old-fashioned, Ma. It wasn't as golden and special as we all thought. Isn't that funny?

OLIVIA: I suppose.

MARY JANE: I was walking past the fairgrounds and I could picture where everything would be and the crowds of people that would come and I could almost smell the sausage the ladies'd make. And you know, it may be changed a lot, but it's not all gone. There's so much here I can rediscover, even. I was realizing that today and I was so happy Ma, cause I was thinking that this year I'm gonna be here for the fair. It's only a month away. A month from tomorrow exactly.

OLIVIA: Is it?

MARY JANE: And maybe I'll take Daddy's place and I'll work in the beer tent this year. And you can visit me every night. I bet I can meet men that way, huh?

OLIVIA: Maybe. We'll see.

MARY JANE: How many years do you think Daddy worked the fair?

OLIVIA: Well, a lot.

MARY JANE: Probably forty.

OLIVIA: Oh, I'm sure.

MARY JANE: Wow. *(Pause.)* Wow. It's so quiet here tonight, isn't it?

OLIVIA: It's been like that. Sometimes I lose track of the time of day and I end up walking around this house alone at three in the morning. I get the times all mixed up.

MARY JANE: Well, that's one reason it's good to have me home.

OLIVIA: Mm-hmm.

MARY JANE: I'm glad I'm here, anyway.

OLIVIA: There's no reason for you to be in California anymore.

MARY JANE: It's more than that. This was the best thing for me to do. It was really the best, you know? I'm glad you asked me to come back.

OLIVIA: Well, you wanted to. It was your idea.

MARY JANE: I think you asked.

OLIVIA: Okay, I'm wrong I suppose.

MARY JANE: Never mind. I'm here. That's all that matters. But I'm planning on getting out and finding a job soon.

OLIVIA: Things are so expensive here.

MARY JANE: I know that, Ma. I'm gonna get a nice job. Maybe in that new office park across from the Mall.

OLIVIA: Well, you could work anywhere.

MARY JANE: I know.

OLIVIA: That's the great thing about being young. You can just pick up and go.

MARY JANE: What are you sayin?

OLIVIA: Nothing.

MARY JANE: You're saying something.

OLIVIA: No. *(Pause.)* The other night I was in the Shop-Rite and I ran into Mrs. Harris and her youngest girl. She's getting married and they're looking for their first house.

MARY JANE: Yeah?

OLIVIA: They've been looking and looking all over town. So I said you should come look at mine, I have exactly what you're trying to find.

MARY JANE: What?

OLIVIA: She was so thrilled. She took my hands and said, "Mrs. Dunn, I always loved your house from the outside when I used to pass it every day on my way to school."

MARY JANE: It's a development. They all look exactly the same.

OLIVIA: She said there was always something special about it. She remembered the white candles I'd put in the window at Christmas and the plastic life-size witch I'd hang on the front door at Halloween to scare all the kids. She said, "Mrs. Dunn. It's a dream come true for me to have your house. I wouldn't do a thing to it." I was so flattered.

MARY JANE: What?

OLIVIA: So they're coming to take a look around.

MARY JANE: Mother.

OLIVIA: Well, I never said I was happy here.

MARY JANE: You didn't say anything.

OLIVIA: Then you should've asked me.

MARY JANE: But I didn't know there was anything wrong.

OLIVIA: How could you not know? How could you think I could stay here? That's just silly. You're just being silly now. Of course can't stay here.

MARY JANE: I just can't believe this. There's no reason for this.

OLIVIA: No reason? Tell my friends that. Call them up and tell them there's no reason to leave and that they should all come back. That it doesn't cost too much to heat a house here and the taxes aren't too high here, that we're not too old and our husbands aren't really gone now and we can all sit on the back porch and eat potato salad and hamburgers again and not know when it's all going to end.

MARY JANE: It didn't end. Don't say that. I know things are different now. I can see that. I'm not blind. But we have to stay right here, Ma.

OLIVIA: Okay. What are you gonna do when we starve, then? Throw me away?

MARY JANE: What? Mother!

OLIVIA: Life is too hard here.

MARY JANE: It's hard everywhere. It's harder out there. Where do you even think we're gonna go? I don't know where on earth you think we're gonna go.

OLIVIA: I don't know.

MARY JANE: You don't know. Great. Well, you should think of someplace to go. You can't sell this house without some idea of where you plan on ending up. Even I know that.

OLIVIA: Tennessee.

MARY JANE: So you decided. Why do you always keep secrets? You always just sit with your mouth closed and nobody ever knows what you're thinking.

OLIVIA: I don't have to tell you everything.

MARY JANE: You were always like this. Always like this. I was nineteen years old and you coulda stopped me from going to California with Jimbo to begin with and my life woulda—

OLIVIA: Nobody coulda stopped you.

MARY JANE: You didn't even try! I was your daughter and you didn't care where I ended up.

OLIVIA: That's ridiculous. You didn't care where you ended up.

MARY JANE: Oh right, of course, you're Miss Innocent again, Ma.

OLIVIA: Oh, I'm Miss Innocent? You make one mistake after another for twenty years and you never took responsibility for one second! You brought babies into this world that you could barely feed cause that husband a yours couldn't hold down a job.

MARY JANE: That's such a lie! How could you say that?

OLIVIA: (Overlapping.) Oh, keep your voice down.

MARY JANE: (Overlapping.) He got laid off that time, Ma! Laid off!
   (Olivia jumps up and shuts the windows.)

OLIVIA: (Overlapping.) You don't have to broadcast it to the world.

MARY JANE: (Overlapping.) And we woulda paid back every penny of that money but Daddy said it was okay not to. Okay not to! You hear me, Ma?

OLIVIA: (Overlapping.) The whole neighborhood can hear you!

MARY JANE: (Overlapping.) So don't you ever bring that up again!

OLIVIA: (Overlapping.) You should be ashamed of that fresh mouth of yours.

MARY JANE: That's all you care about, isn't it? What the neighbors think and where the neighbors are moving to. This is my second chance. I don't know where I'm gonna go now. You're turning my life upside down.

OLIVIA: You don't have any idea what it means to have your life turned upside down.

MARY JANE: That's ridiculous. That's so utterly ridiculous.

OLIVIA: I can't believe you're doin this to me.

MARY JANE: I can't believe you're doin this to me. I guess my plans don't matter. Do they? The failure daughter comes home but that's just not good enough for you, I guess.

OLIVIA: Just shut up. Shut up.

MARY JANE: You shut up. You just shut up forever. How about that? *(She rushes into the bedroom.)* I'm so sick of this. *(She returns with a suitcase, throws it on the floor. She goes back again and retrieves some clothes and things. She throws them on top of the suitcase.)*

OLIVIA: What are you doing?

MARY JANE: What's it matter? It so obviously doesn't matter to you. *(Mary Jane packs.)*

OLIVIA: Okay. Okay. You do what you have to. I'm not gonna keep you here. Leave your mother to do everything herself. Just go ahead and go.

MARY JANE: I am.

OLIVIA: Where do you think you're gonna go?

MARY JANE: I don't know.

(Olivia's up and trying to stop Mary Jane.)

OLIVIA: Just stop it.

(They fight over the suitcase.)

OLIVIA: Stop it now!

MARY JANE: No!

OLIVIA: Stop! Let go. Be a big girl now.

MARY JANE: Give me my stuff!

OLIVIA: Come on. Let go!

MARY JANE: Ma!!

(She gives up and throws the clothes down. She jumps up and walks away. Olivia quickly unpacks all the clothes and closes the suitcase.)

MARY JANE: I guess I should've stayed in Bakersfield.

OLIVIA: No, Mary Jane.

MARY JANE: Oh yeah? At least I didn't have any dreams to get broken again while I was there. At least I knew I didn't deserve any. I was fine before you called me and told me I did. Why'd I believe you? Huh? Why?

OLIVIA: I meant what I said on the phone. That you should start again. I meant that.

MARY JANE: I thought this time you were gonna help me.

OLIVIA: I can't help you.

MARY JANE: But Ma. I can't go back to California. I don't have any money to go anywhere. As soon as you called me and ASKED me to come here I started thinking about all kinds of things and it started looking up again. Coming back kind of washed away all my mistakes. I can't explain it but it did. It did.

OLIVIA: Don't be silly.

MARY JANE: I'm not being silly.

OLIVIA: Well you're not making any sense. I hope you don't go around talking to people like this.

MARY JANE: I don't.

OLIVIA: You're young and strong. That's all that matters.

MARY JANE: I'm not that young.

OLIVIA: You can do whatever you want. You don't have the worries that I have in my head morning noon and night.

MARY JANE: What worries?

OLIVIA: Oh, I don't know. I don't know.
(*Olivia sits on the couch and picks up her cross-stitch. Her hands shake and she can't concentrate but she pretends. She cries.*)

MARY JANE: (*Impatiently.*) Don't cry, Ma.

OLIVIA: I'm not crying. I have never cried in front of my child.
(*They sit in silence.*)

MARY JANE: I like being back here, you know. And it's good to be around all the memories of Daddy. And when my boys come and visit there's room for them, you know? Zachary will get leave from the army and maybe he'll come and visit. And Nathaniel might start making good money in Wyoming and wanna come to New Jersey and see us. Maybe with that new girlfriend. Please, Ma. Things are gonna be easier now, for both of us.

OLIVIA: Nobody said things were supposed to be easy. (*Beat.*) My poor mother…she had it so hard.

MARY JANE: Grandma did? How?

OLIVIA: Well there was a Depression, Mary Jane, don't you know anything?

MARY JANE: Yes I know there was a Depression, but how did I know it affected Grandma?

OLIVIA: It affected everybody. Is that what I sent you to Catholic school for? They didn't teach you anything.

MARY JANE: Well, excuse me.

OLIVIA: Your Grandmother had her cross to bear with two little girls and no food and my father dead. We were starving. All three of us. The landlady put us out. She woke us up real early one Sunday morning and put us out on the streets of New York City.

MARY JANE: What?

OLIVIA: So I said, "What are we gonna do, Mother?" And she said, "First we go to Mass. It is Sunday." I was afraid I was going to go to Hell cause I knelt down in church and blessed myself while at the same time I was thinking what are we doing here this can't help us.

MARY JANE: This really happened?

OLIVIA: My mother asked at the rectory for food and blankets to sleep in the park but they shut the door right on us. I thought God was punishing me, maybe he was. We slept in Central Park that night with nothing. And the whole time I'm waiting for my trip to Hell cause I was sure it was coming. My mother and me and Aunt Carol walked the streets all day and we weren't talking. And finally my mother took us up on the George Washington Bridge. The three of us were sitting up on the bridge all afternoon and I had no idea why. And finally my mother said, "See the water? If you hold on to mother as tight as you can we can all go into the water and we'll be together forever with Jesus."

MARY JANE: Ma.

OLIVIA: And Carol started to cry. Mother said, "Jesus loves us. Jesus loves us. You will never be hungry again." We were starving to death and I knew it. So we all held on real tight together and walked to the edge of the bridge, but I let go. Cause I knew I wouldn't get to Heaven with them. And Grandma couldn't jump off that bridge without both her girls. By then a man in a car stopped and he gave my mother a half dollar to feed us.

MARY JANE: He saved your life.

OLIVIA: Well it worked out fine, Mary Jane. We went to a luncheonette on the New Jersey side. And she called her first cousin who had married a man from the south and moved to Tennessee. Her cousin had no money but they said, "We have a farm and can feed ourselves. So if you send your girls we can feed them too." So me and my sister went on a train to live with strangers. I thought it was heaven. Green and blue everywhere I looked, and we could pick crab apples and sink our teeth right in them. (Beat.) We didn't see our mother for eight years. It was very hard. As soon as I got back up here and lived with Grandma in New Jersey, I met Daddy and went off and got married. Carol stayed with Grandma, though, for a few years.

MARY JANE: I can't believe this story. Why didn't you ever tell me?

OLIVIA: It's not the kind of thing you go around telling people about.

MARY JANE: Telling people? I'm your daughter.

OLIVIA: Well, whatever, Mary Jane.

MARY JANE: You told me now. Today. Why'd you tell me now?

OLIVIA: It came up.

MARY JANE: You wanted me to know. You told me cause you wanted me to know.

(Pause. Mary Jane sits and thinks. Olivia suddenly opens up.)

OLIVIA: You know, I was scared of the ocean my whole life. But when you were four and we took you down the shore you took one look at the water and said, "Mommy, I'm gonna have to go out there." And I said, "Oh no, Mary Jane, those waves are gonna knock you down." And you said, "I know they will but I'll get right back up again and swim hard." And that's just what you did.

MARY JANE: Really? *(Pause.)* You know why I left? You're not gonna believe it when I tell you. I really wanted to live in a van. A light blue Chevy van with white trim. But Jimbo didn't listen to me he got a black van. But, I figured—it's still a van. It was the only thing I really wanted. Can you believe that my only goal was to live in a van? You said to me when I was leaving, "What is goin on in your head?" And I made up all this stuff, but that was it. That was all I was thinking.

OLIVIA: How on earth did you come up with an idea like that one? You can't shower or go to the bathroom or cook a meal on a van.

MARY JANE: Well, that's true. *(Beat.)* It's good to talk like this.

OLIVIA: People talk too much these days. They think it solves the world's problems.

MARY JANE: But you can tell people what you want. You can tell me. You know. What's going on in your head.

OLIVIA: I want to go home. I can't do it alone. When Daddy died you said you were comin. Back to New Jersey. I thought oh, now I have someone again. Someone to take me home.

MARY JANE: Oh, Ma.

OLIVIA: I'm sorry.

MARY JANE: No. Don't say you're sorry. I don't want you to ever say you're sorry to me. *(She sits near her mother.)* It's okay, Ma. It's okay. *(She takes Olivia's cross stitch into her hands.)* Oh, this is so nice.

OLIVIA: It's a house. I bought it in the crafts store but I changed the colors of the thread myself, to green and white. To stand for our house.

MARY JANE: Yeah. It's really beautiful.

OLIVIA: Well I try.

(An ice cream truck rings its bell.)

MARY JANE: An ice cream truck? *(She gets up and goes to the front door and opens it.)* There's still an ice cream truck.

OLIVIA: Why don't you go get some? Go ahead, stop him.

MARY JANE: Okay. I think I will. *(She stops and turns back toward her mother.)* Ma, remember the song we'd sing? *(Sing-song.)* "SAM! SAM! The Good Humor man!" All the kids would sing for Sam to stop.

OLIVIA: And your father! He loved to sing that song too. You could hear him all the way up the street.

MARY JANE: Are you kidding, you could hear him a mile a way. *(Mary Jane has stopped, stares out the screen door.)*

OLIVIA: Well you better run!

MARY JANE: No, I don't wanna. I'd rather just remember it.

OLIVIA: Well. You won't get any ice cream that way.

(Mary Jane stares out the door, memorizing her old neighborhood.)

MARY JANE: That's okay. *(Pause.)* The best thing about anyplace is remembering it.

(Neighborhood sounds get louder.)

MARY JANE: I like to remember everything exactly. *(Pause.)* Hear that lawnmower? I love that sound.

OLIVIA: Yeah, I suppose that's a nice sound. *(She thinks.)* Comforting. Isn't it?

MARY JANE: *(Still staring out.)* Yeah. It's comforting. *(She looks to her mother. Beat.)* We'll go to Tennessee. Me and you. And we'll be home. *(Looking out the door.)* We'll be home.

THE END

The Observatory

BY GREG GERMANN

THE AUTHOR

Greg Germann is an actor who has performed both on and off Broadway working with such playwrights as Lanford Wilson, John Guare, Neil Simon, and Stephen Sondheim. He has worked extensively in television and film. He wrote, directed, and starred in *Pete's Garden* that was excepted into competition at the Sundance Film Festival. *The Observatory* marks Mr. Germann's debut as a playwright. It is published by Dramatists Play Service.

ORIGINAL PRODUCTION

The Observatory was originally produced at The Ensemble Theatre Studio, June 1996. It was directed by Jim Simpson; the set design was by Bruce Goodrich; the costume design was by Murell Horton; the lighting design was by Greg MacPherson; the sound design was by Jeffrey Taylor; and stage manager was Alicina Vilankulu. The cast was as follows:

Roman . . . . Dennis Boutsikaris
Alice . . . . Diana LaMar

The author would like to thank Christine Mourad for her invaluable support.

(As the lights go to black we hear the voice of a...)

FIDDLE PLAYER: *(Voice over.)* Okay let's try it. One, two...

(Then an accordion and a fiddle make their way through a Celtic waltz. The melody is sweet, but these musicians need more than a little practice. Then they stop abruptly mid-phrase. Still in the black.)

FIDDLE PLAYER: *(Voice over.)* No, no, no. And again.

(Another effort and they fall apart.)

FIDDLE PLAYER: *(Voice over.)* A "D." It's a "D."

(One last try, but it's no use.)

FIDDLE PLAYER: *(Voice over.)* No, no, no. Forget it. Let's...take a break.

(At the same moment the lights bounce up revealing Alice sitting on a crude stone foundation of an ancient dilapidated gazebo. This antiquated 'watchtower' has seen better days. A structure of some kind is currently being built on it. Alice stares out at the audience. We're on a knoll overlooking the Hudson River Valley. A long beat.)

ALICE: This is a magical spot. It's perfect really. *(Silence. She inhales deeply.)* You can actually feel the power of it.

(A crash of two-by-fours offstage.)

ROMAN: *(Offstage.)* It was right here—

ALICE: It's amazing. This place. Here. Not over here, or here, but right here, is different than any other because of what will take place on this spot.

(Silence. Again, two by fours.)

ROMAN: *(Off.)* God, I can't...

ALICE: Or has taken place. I mean it is already.

(Roman enters looking all over for something.)

ROMAN: AHH...

ALICE: It doesn't need something to make it what it is already.

ROMAN: I can't find the—

ALICE: It's sacred. It's hallowed ground. We're drawn here. Something mysterious. Some force. Something intangible.

ROMAN: The view.

ALICE: I don't want to impose my ego on it. It doesn't need my ego. It exists already. It doesn't need me. It doesn't need our little parade to give it its, I don't know, its what, its...?

ROMAN: View.

(Roman stops. Alice pulls a tape measure in and out while she ruminates. He takes it from her.)

ALICE: Not religious, that would be...it's bigger, it's bigger than God, it's...

ROMAN: There's something bigger?

ALICE: Yes. The universe. The laws of the universe. It's impossible to accentu-
ate, or...

ROMAN: To what?

ALICE: To, uh, enunciate...?

ROMAN: Articulate?

ALICE: Yeah, to "say."

ROMAN: *(Slowly.)* V-i-e-w.
(Beat.)

ALICE: It's like Stone Henge, or the Pyramids, or...have you ever been to
Santa Fe?

ROMAN: Santa Fe...?

ALICE: Yeah, in New Mexico.

ROMAN: I know, but Sante Fe—

ALICE: It's such a powerful place. There's a feeling there. You're just drawn. Do
you believe in that?

ROMAN: In what?

ALICE: The reality of that? That reality?

ROMAN: That people are "drawn" to Santa Fe?

ALICE: I'm sure there's tons of reasons why people go—

ROMAN: I don't know if I would say people are "drawn" to there, "drawn" to
Santa Fe, I—

ALICE: Not all people, some people, some people feel a pull or they just know
that that's a place for them to go, or—

ROMAN: Yeah, but I wouldn't say that people are "pulled" either—

ALICE: I'm not saying against their will or whatever, just that—

ROMAN: People go there, okay, but I wouldn't—

ALICE: Right, but they go with a sense of purpose or—

ROMAN: —make too much out of it. *(Silence. Roman works.)* There's
turquoise.

ALICE: What?

ROMAN: If you like turquoise, but...
(Roman measures. Alice jumps up.)

ALICE: I don't care. Why should I care? I care about what's important. *There
are so many.*

ROMAN: So many...?

ALICE: Oh God yes! Infinite. When I just think about the ones I know. Or
the ones I think I know, or thought I *knew. I thought I knew*...but now
I've made a choice. 'Reality' is so subjective. I just don't care.

ROMAN: What other people think?

ALICE: Reality. Whose reality. I have to be an independent thinker. An independent experiencer. There is simply not time in the day to be "self conscious" about it.

ROMAN: About what? I have no—

ALICE: It may not be real. So what? "Real." Not "real." Who has the time? You know Benjamin?

ROMAN: Benjamin…?

ALICE: Benjamin Arron. He's Thomas's best friend.

ROMAN: Right, the caterer. He's catering the reception.

ALICE: Well now he owns "Benjamin's."

ROMAN: "Benjamin's"…?

ALICE: Oh, it's four stars. It is now. The head chef is from "Tables," which was four star, but now I don't know. *(Laughs.)* Benjamin raided the kitchen so—

ROMAN: …"Tables"…?

ALICE: So he probably wiped it right off the map, right off the menu. Benjamin is so aggressive. He's an animal. Just ruthless. I've learned so much from him.

ROMAN: Learned what?

ALICE: He's a very important friend. He's so present.

ROMAN: Learned what?

ALICE: I'm lucky that way. I know so many people who are "there," not in a clichéd way, but just "there." Present.

ROMAN: Learned what?

ALICE: To be there. To experience. I think his reality is so close to mine. Not identical. *(She finds this terribly funny.)* How could it be? But close. Parallel. Some people you feel that your reality is parallel and some you feel it's,…perpendicular, or…Benjamin's is parallel. He took me, with Stuart Press and Margo, to the opening of "Salvation" and despite all of the hoopla—

ROMAN: Wait, wait, wait. "Salvation," what is "Salvation"? I have no—

ALICE: It's absolutely the most amazing place. It's nouvelle East European, but all organic. It's Stewart's place, at least he's a partner with Glennon Fasche.

ROMAN: Stewart…?

ALICE: Stewart Press. Stewart's the lead in André's new film, *The Mensa Factor*.

ROMAN: Oh, right, that movie that's like five hours long or something—

ALICE: Oh God! It is ground breaking. It changed me. It was one of those life changing nights. I was with Sylvia Thayer and her son and all three of us just sat stunned in the theatre for twenty minutes. Speechless. He takes the medium, the medium of the twentieth century and just molds it, bends it with his will. A filmmaker at his peak. There is simply nothing to say about it. *(Pause.)* I've thought of it so often, since. *(Pause.)* Sometimes... *(Pause.)* I'm sorry,...it cuts me so, deeply. *(Cries.)* God, oh god we are so lucky. The people. The experience. We go through life, stumbling, groping, desperate for some hint that there is a possibility of sense to be made from all of this and then a film, or a friend or a,...restaurant, just the act of... *(Sighs.)* God...

(Pause.)

ROMAN: The act of...what?

ALICE: What act?

ROMAN: You said a restaurant and just the act of, something...?

ALICE: Oh,...of, eating or...you know.

ROMAN: I have no idea what you're—

ALICE: I was just saying that when Benjamin took me with Stuart and Margo to "Salvation," the reality that he creates is just so alive, it's so,...real, it's just so—

ROMAN: Yeah, see, I have no idea what you're—

ALICE: Oh, it's just that you create reality. Reality isn't real, I mean like a real thing, it's something, or actually it's nothing, I mean it's only the thing you decide *you* want it to be, so Benjamin's reality, or what he calls his—

ROMAN: No. Let me rephrase that; not only do I have no idea *what* you're talking about and no clue who these people are, I don't care. I don't care about the subject and I don't care about these...people. *(Pause. Roman works.)*

ALICE: You have so much integrity.

ROMAN: Because I'm out of work?

ALICE: It's heroic. What you did.

ROMAN: Oh, I thought I was a quitter.

ALICE: Exactly. People are cowards, and when they are forced to watch someone break away from the flock of cowards, they show their colors. Because under the light of one truthful act no one can hide, but they try. Oh my god, they will do or say anything.

ROMAN: So this sudden, or all too gradual shift of my fortune is a result of "one truthful act?"

ALICE: Of course. Of course. That's the other side of it. The cost. The cost that no one can stand to see. Truth is not free. You pay. You pay and you pay beyond understanding.

ROMAN: And I've paid?

ALICE: Oh yes.

ROMAN: Beyond understanding?

ALICE: You've fallen.

ROMAN: Except you.

ALICE: Except…?

ROMAN: You understand?

ALICE: I pretend to.

ROMAN: You don't?

ALICE: I do, but I can never really know.

ROMAN: Oh.

ALICE: Not really.

ROMAN: Maybe you're right.

> *(Pause.)*

ALICE: The power of gesture.

ROMAN: The what?

ALICE: I was thinking of that statue by Rodin of the town officials that surrender to the king as human ransom so their town would be spared. He
sculpted each one of them, in the moment of their greatest bravery, but
depicted them as scared and pitiful. So, the city officials who commissioned the work rejected his miniature because they said that their
heroes should look more fearless and noble, but Rodin refused saying he
would only depict what the moment cost them. *(Very simply Alice
assumes a pose of anguish.)* That's how I understand you.

ROMAN: Scared and pitiful.

ALICE: No. You've stood up for what you believe.

> *(Silence. Roman works.)*

ALICE: We are so much alike.

ROMAN: Is that bad for you or for me?

ALICE: You like to work with your hands.

ROMAN: This?

ALICE: Yes. Physical labor is so underestimated.

ROMAN: I never underestimated it.

ALICE: Oh God, I agree.

ROMAN: With what? I didn't—

ALICE: I love to just work, you know? To labor. To sweat. To make something
with my hands. The world is so "ready made."

ROMAN: It's a pain in the ass.

ALICE: It is! It is! It takes such effort to be conscious when everything is set before you ready to wear, ready to eat, ready to buy, buy, buy, buy, buy.

ROMAN: No. This. This is a pain in the ass. It takes too long and I don't have any idea what I'm doing. If I wasn't broke I'd run out and buy a prefab version of this thing.

ALICE: It's going to be a beautiful altar.

ROMAN: It's a headache.

ALICE: That's what makes it meaningful. You didn't just go out and check off some candle sticks that they registered for. You stepped out into the unknown.

ROMAN: Thomas paid for the wood, it was an easy way out.

ALICE: But it's not easy. It's not easy for you. You have no idea what you're doing.

ROMAN: I wouldn't say *no* idea, I—

ALICE: That's what makes it beautiful. It's a beautiful thing.

ROMAN: If you're into abstract art.

ALICE: Theresa is very moved.

ROMAN: She can afford to be moved.

ALICE: It's a very moving gift.

ROMAN: Look they're gonna stand up there for ten minutes tomorrow and then this thing will just start rotting along with the rest of this place.

ALICE: The "observatory."

ROMAN: A misnomer.

ALICE: It's not. One of Thomas's ancestors was an amateur astronomer, Edmond or Ellery or somebody, and—

ROMAN: I know. You told me the whole story how he went nuts and all he ever built was this pathetic gazebo—

ALICE: He wasn't nuts—

ROMAN: —so Thomas's forefathers never watched the stars, they only watched their ships.

ALICE: He wasn't "nuts," he was an atheist, and he—

ROMAN: First in a long line.

ALICE: —was ostracized, and I think it's romantic or inspiring that somebody—

ROMAN: What that Thomas wasn't the first dilettante in his family, or that he and Theresa have genetic insanity in common as well as little else?

(*Beat.*)

ALICE: I just have no idea what to give them.

ROMAN: They're sort of set for life.

ALICE: They want so little.

ROMAN: Buy Thomas a new pair of shoes.

ALICE: *(Laughs.)* He really lives it.

ROMAN: Lives what?

ALICE: I don't know, his shoes. He doesn't just talk about it.
      (Beat.)

ROMAN: He "lives it," because of his shoes? Because he's worn the same pair of shoes for five years?

ALICE: Eight. He got them right after Theresa and I started working for him.

ROMAN: That *is* insanity. What's he trying to prove? That he takes extremely fine care of his shoes?

ALICE: He lives it.

ROMAN: Lives it? Lives what? He's got like a hundred acres on the Hudson River, a two-hundred-and-fifty-year-old estate, more money than God, but he won't change his shoes.

ALICE: Exactly. He runs this huge foundation, the artists retreat, the Return the Earth conference, outreach programs, but he puts these practices into his daily life, right down to the shoes on his feet.

ROMAN: How do his shoes contribute to the—

ALICE: Ecology. The Return the Earth Conference. He doesn't just go to the meetings, he really—

ROMAN: "Return the Earth." Come on, this whole save the earth. Return the earth. It's just insulting. As if we can "save" it or "return" it. We never had it. It's incredible.

ALICE: But we can, if we—

ROMAN: This place has been bombarded by intergalactic rocks, flooded, and blown apart from the inside out, it can certainly withstand the impact of Thomas's Hush Puppies! Of course Thomas and The Return the Earth people descended from a long line of atheists, don't believe in "something more powerful," like God, am I even allowed to say it, which is why the thing's called Save The Earth in the first place and not save our big ass!!

ALICE: I just—

ROMAN: It's just simplistic. Hence, Thomas will put on the same pair of shoes for the rest of his life. I just feel bad for my sister.

ALICE: For Theresa…?

ROMAN: Can you imagine what those Hush Puppies smell like?

ALICE: You have to admire Thomas.

ROMAN: Why, because he's saving my sister from a pathetic life in a one room walk-up with two cats on 105th Street?

ALICE: She tried to be an artist, just because she's suffered or wasn't given the opportunities she deserved—

ROMAN: She never suffered because she was an "artist," she suffered and now has given up because she refused to accept the requirements of the real world.

ALICE: She's not giving up, she's moving on, evolving, using her talent and intellect in the "real world" to—

ROMAN: Is she writing? No. Was she a writer? Yes. Has she given up being a writer, an "artist"? Yes.

ALICE: Whose real world? What are the requirements of the real world?

ROMAN: She "suffered," she was in misery not because she was an artist, but because she refused to grasp the fact that she could write a wall full of fiction and if no one wanted to read it, it's meaningless. In the real world there's a marketplace. In the real world if a tree falls in the forest and no one hears it...WHO GIVES A SHIT! That's the real world!

ALICE: So someone working in oblivion without recognition for a lifetime should just hang it up and walk away. Van Gogh or Emily Dickenson, should have just walked away,—

ROMAN: God, no, no, not Van Gogh! Don't give me Van Gogh! Van Gogh, that's so predictable!

ALICE: He's not predictable, he's an inspiration, he's—

ROMAN: People pull out Van Gogh when they're trying to prove an artist has to be insane and destitute to be worthwhile. It's cheap.

ALICE: He suffered, he worked in oblivion, he—

ROMAN: Look. I love Van Gogh, I love his paintings, I love that song about that painting, I love the whole thing with the ear and the girl, but we're talking about Theresa. The fact is she gets depressed. Clinically depressed. She was in trouble, and if marrying Thomas is more effective than medication I'm all for it. We're talking about her will, her choice—

ALICE: No we're not. We're not. We're talking about her way of life. We're talking about *me*. I live in a one room walk-up. I don't have cats, but if I wasn't allergic I—

ROMAN: I'm not talking about—

ALICE: We are. We are. That's okay. We can talk about me. I like to talk about me.

ROMAN: I don't want to talk about you.

ALICE: Then we're talking about you.

ROMAN: I don't want to talk about me.

ALICE: But we are, we are.

ROMAN: No we're—

ALICE: *(Enjoying this.)* This is the way we always go at it.

ROMAN: We're not going at anything—

ALICE: I just love it!

ROMAN: Love what?

ALICE: This. There's this force that just pulls us together even though we're just on the opposite side of, well, of everything!

ROMAN: This isn't about politics.

ALICE: Exactly. This is what happened to us the last time we were up here.
(Beat.)

ROMAN: No, no, no, that was different, I was not clear, it was—

ALICE: It was inevitable, we needed—

ROMAN: —it was my fault, I—

ALICE: —to be taken in—

ROMAN: —was under all this pressure from the new job and—

ALICE: —I needed to be seen and you—

ROMAN: —my marriage was already—

ALICE: —you needed someone to believe in you. *(Beat. Matter of fact.)* I just believed in you.
(Long silence. Roman begins to work again.)

ALICE: Lust.

ROMAN: The what…?

ALICE: Pure sexual energy.

ROMAN: Between us?

ALICE: This pure appetite.
(Beat.)

ROMAN: Can you hand me the level.

ALICE: Because I'm a person, a woman, controlled absolutely by appetite. I'm just ravenous, I'm a ravenous person.

ROMAN: Could you please hand me the level.

ALICE: I'm working with a healer. She's actually a therapist, but she uses holistic healing methods. It's very intense. She "sees" this tremendous, repressed sexual energy in me. I'm making real strides to embrace it.

ROMAN: This is not a level.

ALICE: —It's always been like that with men. This sexual energy just pours out of me, it's just that I don't—

ROMAN: *(Finally picks up the level himself.)* This. This is a level.

(Beat.)

ALICE: You've had a lot of turmoil.

ROMAN: I prefer "changes."

(Beat.)

ALICE: I wasn't surprised.

ROMAN: About what?

ALICE: That you came back.

ROMAN: My sister's getting married.

ALICE: It's more complicated—

ROMAN: What, my marriage, my job, what?

ALICE: All of it. So we meet again here on this spot. It's mysterious and simple, and complicated and—

ROMAN: It doesn't seem complicated to me.

ALICE: Well it's not, I just wasn't surprised.

ROMAN: About what!?

ALICE: All of it.

ROMAN: All of what?

ALICE: Well, your job.

ROMAN: That I quit?

ALICE: Absolutely. I didn't read your pieces except the last one, which was just so pained, just full of pain, but it must have been a very empty job.

ROMAN: Working for a nationally recognized newspaper that gave me the career opportunity of a lifetime?

ALICE: No, I was excited, but then they forced you to express opinions that are so narrow and—

ROMAN: But you didn't read the pieces.

ALICE: No but Theresa would tell me. It sounded just—

ROMAN: But you didn't read them.

ALICE: It was so hard. To think of you being forced to—

ROMAN: I wasn't forced to do anything. I wrote about what I wanted to. I said exactly what I wanted to say. Where do you get this thing that I was forced?

ALICE: I knew you were trying to get somewhere. It just broke my heart that you had to compromise your beliefs to go there.

ROMAN: Compromise?! I never compromised. Jesus!

ALICE: I just thought when you quit, like you said in that last piece, "…a crisis of conscience…" that you—

ROMAN: Oh, I see, I see. You figured they were forcing me to wax poetic for their conservative agenda and finally I couldn't take living the lie.

ALICE: God no, not that you were lying, you wouldn't lie. It's like you were compromised, you made a compromise.

(Roman stops working.)

ROMAN: Would you?

ALICE: What?

ROMAN: Lie?

ALICE: About what?

ROMAN: What you believe in?

ALICE: Why would you do that?

ROMAN: You think if you just "believe" that'll do the trick?

ALICE: That's the whole point of believing in something.

ROMAN: You think anything would ever get done if people didn't negotiate, didn't make compromises?

ALICE: That's the problem, everything is compromised and watered down until it's meaningless.

ROMAN: So you're a radical.

ALICE: You have to draw the line.

ROMAN: Oh like your heroes André and Thomas.

ALICE: Yes. Yes. My God, the final movement of André's film, *The Mensa Factor*—

ROMAN: *(Overlapping, "The Mensa Factor*—") That would be in hour nineteen!

ALICE: —is about a man who loses everything for what he believes. It's based on Thomas' ancestor the amateur astronomer. This man, the character, stands up to his family and these politicians because he refuses to be homogenized and conform.

ROMAN: He draws the line.

ALICE: Yes. The film is an indictment of this country's relentless effort to homogenize and erase individuality.

ROMAN: Wait! Whose individuality are we erasing?

ALICE: My God, everybody who comes to this country. We demand they give up what makes them unique.

ROMAN: Which is what?

ALICE: Their identity. Their ethnic identity. Their myths and history.

ROMAN: What about our myths?

ALICE: Our myths? You and I? What happened between—?

ROMAN: No, this country. We have myths.

ALICE: *This* country? Myths? What myths?

ROMAN: We got a thousand myths. We got the myth about uh,…what about,

uh…the, uh…Washington. The myth of Washington as the indispens-
able man of moral strength who cannot tell a lie. There's a myth.
(Beat. She considers this.)

ALICE: Right. Okay, that's a myth. That's a good myth.

ROMAN: Absolutely. It is. It's a good myth.

ALICE: But what about their identity, their ethnic identity?

ROMAN: Oh, so every day becomes a national holiday because everybody's cel-
ebrating their own ethnicity. So we end up replacing *our* moral stan-
dards, by creating and reinforcing this bogus self esteem.

ALICE: Exactly. So we shove our "morality" down the world's throat.

ROMAN: Just the part of the world that wants to live here.

ALICE: You can't force people to live by our morality.

ROMAN: We sure can. You impose morality by establishing limits on behav-
ior. It's called "laws."

ALICE: That's the point in André's film.—

ROMAN: Enough about André.

ALICE: —It's the point of what you did. You didn't break any laws and still
you lose everything.

ROMAN: I didn't lose—

ALICE: God, André illuminates *your* struggle with a two-hundred-year-old
event. He's just brilliant.

ROMAN: Brilliant, why? Becasue he makes a movie about the evils of western
science that lasts half a day and some institutional video on how to burn
the flag?

ALICE: *(Excited.)* Oh my God! *Flagday!* You've seen *Flagday!?*

ROMAN: People used to send me all kinds of crap.

ALICE: I would kill to see that.

ROMAN: Life's too short.

ALICE: I just think we may have to reject politicians and politics as a realistic
method for substantial subversive change.

ROMAN: You are a radical.

ALICE: We have to look deeper. Towards art and spirituality.*(Beat.)* That's
what I want to do.

ROMAN: Look deeper?

ALICE: What you did.

ROMAN: What did I do?

ALICE: Shed some light.

ROMAN: I shed light?

ALICE: I know, I'm not a writer or anything. *I'm* very visual. I have this idea.

It's just this image, you know. Not even a whole story. I'm a very visual person. Language is so restrictive. It's not universal, it only scratches the surface. It's just not necessary anymore. It doesn't have the power to inspire or move us the way that images do now.

ROMAN: Oh. So you want to make a movie?

ALICE: A film. Oh yeah. Film. Film is the medium of the future. I don't think people read anymore.

ROMAN: *(Enjoying her.)* That's right you're still on strike?

ALICE: On strike?

ROMAN: I remember you said you were on strike, against the media. I liked that.

ALICE: That was just an exercise in prioritizing time. This is about taking back the tools of creation.

ROMAN: Oh. So you're taking something back…?

ALICE: Language, the written word, holds the tools of the creative spirit hostage. I think we could be returning to a primitive time when everyone has access to a universal language. When everyone knew how to paint, sing, and dance. I just think language is dead.

(Roman starts to speak, but…Long silence.)

ROMAN: So it'll be a silent movie? *(Quickly correcting.)* Film.

ALICE: …What?

ROMAN: The movie you—

(This cracks them both up.)

ALICE: Oh. God. You're so funny. Right. *(She can't stop laughing.)* No, people will talk, I mean they have to.

ROMAN: So it'll be a "talkie?"

ALICE: People have to talk. There's no way around that.

(This makes them laugh even harder. Pause.)

ROMAN: It's frustrating isn't it?

ALICE: What?

ROMAN: People have to talk.

ALICE: *(Thoughtful.)* …It is. It is because—

(Music. A long note as a fiddle tunes to an accordion.)

ALICE: *(Whispers.)* God, that was so…

ROMAN: Because why?

ALICE: That music came from nowhere.

ROMAN: They're not very good.

ALICE: Who?

ROMAN: The two guys Theresa hired to play tomorrow. Because why? Are you…?

ALICE: *(Cries a little.)* There's so much to say, to express.

ROMAN: Are you all right?

ALICE: There is, there is. I'm so relieved that you came back.

ROMAN: Relieved…?

ALICE: Because you have so much to say or to write about.

> *(We hear a few measures of the same waltz from the beginning of the play, played poorly by the accordion and the fiddle.)*

ROMAN: I have a gift for the diatribe. The only thing I'm good for now is talk radio.

ALICE: No. You have ideas and you have belief. And with that lives are changed and the world is made.

> *(Troubled, Roman turns away.)*

ROMAN: What if I am…

ALICE: What?

ROMAN: …drawn to you?

ALICE: …What if…?

ROMAN: What would it mean?

ALICE: There's possibility.

ROMAN: What about—

ALICE: Roman…

ROMAN: —the laws of the universe?

ALICE: *(She goes to him. Gently.)* I can just see you.

ROMAN: *(A little lost.)* What…?

ALICE: Your anguish.

> *(She kisses his hair lightly. The music stops. He lets her kiss him. After a moment he stops her and rises suddenly.)*

ROMAN: This isn't right. You don't know me. *(Beat.)* You've never even read anything I've written.

ALICE: I'm sorry, I know that's really—

ROMAN: I don't care. I mean I really don't care.

ALICE: I should've. Maybe I should read more, I just—

ROMAN: No, I truly could care less. It's just you talk on and on about how similar we are, how we're so pulled together, it's just ridiculous.

ALICE: I know you're in a crisis, that—

ROMAN: You know nothing about my "crisis."

ALICE: I didn't know her well, but—

ROMAN: Who?

ALICE: Marion.

ROMAN: My marriage?!

ALICE: That and everything, it must be—

ROMAN: This is not about my marriage.

ALICE: I did read the last piece and I thought—

ROMAN: You know nothing. It's so presumptuous.

ALICE: I shouldn't have kissed you, I just feel this pull, this—

ROMAN: God! It's ridiculous! I haven't seen you for two years. I barely knew you then. You don't know me! You don't know what I believe! You think language is dead, God is dead, science is evil, politics is useless, progress should be stopped, but art! Art is good! Art will save us! Art will guide us out of the darkness! You've thrown out intellect, reason, and morality and armed yourself with a coloring book! You can barely form a sentence but expect to be heard! It's ridiculous!

(Silence. Roman starts to hammer.)

ALICE: God. *(Alice sighs.)* I just can't help opening up to you—

(Roman slams his thumb with the hammer.)

ROMAN: AHHHH!

ALICE: Oh God! What happened? What did you do? Are you all right?

ROMAN: Damn. *(Roman winces and paces silently.)*

ALICE: Do you want me to get some, I don't know…some ice…?

ROMAN: No. No. No.

ALICE: God that must hurt. Let me see. Let me look.

ROMAN: No. No. No.

ALICE: No. Let me look. Let me see.

ROMAN: No. No.

ALICE: It's all right, just—

ROMAN: No.

ALICE: Here—

ROMAN: No.

ALICE: Let me—

ROMAN: No.

(She begins following him to catch a glance at his wound.)

ALICE: Oh wow, that must really hurt. Oh it looks so painful. It must hurt. God. Does it hurt?

ROMAN: No.

ALICE: It must. It must be intolerable. Let me get some ice.

ROMAN: No. No ice.

ALICE: Ice will help.

ROMAN: No ice.

ALICE: Ice is good.

ROMAN: I don't want ice.

ALICE: Let me—

ROMAN: NO ICE!

ALICE: Are you sure—

ROMAN: NO! Are you deaf?! God!

(*Pause.*)

ALICE: This must be very difficult.

ROMAN: It's fine. It's numb.

ALICE: No. This. A wedding. Now. All these people. Looking at you like you must be suffering.

ROMAN: I'm not suffering.

ALICE: I know. I mean you just don't want a lot of attention or anything.

(*He stares at her. Pause.*)

ALICE: Did she expect it?

ROMAN: What?

ALICE: When you left.

ROMAN: Marion?

ALICE: Yes.

ROMAN: Was she surprised?

ALICE: Yes.

ROMAN: I don't think so.

ALICE: Oh.

ROMAN: She asked me to leave.

ALICE: Oh. (*Pause.*) It was inevitable.

ROMAN: What?

ALICE: This. That you and Marion have, I don't know, run into such…

ROMAN: Why? Why? Why inevitable?

ALICE: Lots of reasons I guess. Just what happened between us, I think I always believed that you'd come back.

ROMAN: For you?

ALICE: Maybe we are drawn together—

ROMAN: You thought I came back here for you?

ALICE: I know there's a lot more to it than that, but—

ROMAN: I did not come back here for you. Jesus.

ALICE: Okay, I was just saying that what happened between us was very—

ROMAN: I came back because I was given a way out. Okay.

ALICE: I'm on your side…

ROMAN: You just have no idea what side I'm on.

ALICE: It doesn't matter.

ROMAN: (*Laughs.*) Exactly. I had a way out. I was given a way out. Okay. That's why I'm here. I did not come back here for you!

ALICE: I know it's not that simple, I just meant—

ROMAN: I came back because I had to leave my job.

ALICE: I know, I read—

ROMAN: You don't know.

ALICE: I do, I read your—

ROMAN: *(Matter of fact.)* I did not *quit*. I *had* to leave my job because I borrowed a few paragraphs and didn't bother to use quotation marks.

ALICE: You what—?

ROMAN: I came back because I had to resign or be branded a empty vessel without an original thought.

ALICE: But I read your—

ROMAN: I came back because I figured a clever way out was to portray myself in my farewell piece as a fallen believer—

ALICE: That's the piece I read, it was very—

ROMAN: —so my last piece, *Crisis of Conscience,* was a lie, an excuse.
(Beat.)

ALICE: So you didn't find, "the viewpoint of this page painfully inconsistent with your own"—

ROMAN: My God! You did! You actually read it.

ALICE: It was very moving.
(Beat.)

ROMAN: I'm sorry.

ALICE: I thought...

ROMAN: I did not come back for you.

ALICE: Oh. *(Beat.)* It must be very painful.

ROMAN: It's fine. *(His thumb.)*

ALICE: No, no. To believe so strongly in something, but pretend that you don't.

ROMAN: It's just pretend.
(Beat.)

ALICE: She said she was worried about you.

ROMAN: Who...?

ALICE: Marion. That she was worried that—

ROMAN: My wife said...?

ALICE: —you lost your moral compass.

ROMAN: She what?

ALICE: That you wouldn't speak to her.

ROMAN: She said...to you?

ALICE: Yes, that's why I thought you left.

ROMAN: You spoke—?

ALICE: She told me you couldn't take it anymore.

ROMAN: You spoke to her?

ALICE: Yes.

ROMAN: When?

ALICE: Last week.

ROMAN: How? Why? Why did you speak?

ALICE: She said she still had hope but she was trying to kill it.

ROMAN: Kill it…? What—?

ALICE: Yes.

ROMAN: No. *Why!?* Why did you speak with her?

ALICE: Why?

ROMAN: Yes. How? She called you?

ALICE: No.

ROMAN: You saw her somewhere? What?

ALICE: No. She seemed angry.

ROMAN: Angry? What? When you spoke?

ALICE: Talking to me made her angry.

ROMAN: Why did you talk to her?

ALICE: I phoned.

ROMAN: You called her?

ALICE: Yes.

ROMAN: For what purpose? Why call her?

ALICE: I wanted to know.

ROMAN: To know what?!

ALICE: If it was over.

ROMAN: My marriage?

ALICE: Yes.

ROMAN: Jesus!

ALICE: I wanted to know.

ROMAN: You called her and asked her if it was over?!

ALICE: Not exactly like that, but—

ROMAN: Jesus!

ALICE: I don't think she ever really knew you.

ROMAN: What did she tell you?

ALICE: We didn't really talk very long.

ROMAN: What did she tell you?

ALICE: I'm not even sure she remembered me. She said she did, but I'm not sure.

ROMAN: What did you talk about?

ALICE: Do you think she remembered me?

ROMAN: What did you talk about?

ALICE: At first, just hello, you know, asking what she's been doing and—

ROMAN: Get to the point! What did she tell you?

ALICE: Nothing. She wasn't coming to the wedding and just what I told you.

ROMAN: You called my wife!

ALICE: I don't think she knows you.

ROMAN: What are you talking about?

ALICE: She's just not like—

ROMAN: Why do you keep saying that?! How do you know she doesn't know me?!

ALICE: Because she said—

ROMAN: How do you know?!

ALICE: She said you lost your moral compass!

ROMAN: Oh God!

ALICE: I told her I just felt that was so predictable.

ROMAN: You what?

ALICE: Someone begins to question what their life means and it's trivialized into losing one to the other side.

ROMAN: You said that to her?

ALICE: If she wasn't so upset I would've really defended you, because I thought what you did is so—

ROMAN: You didn't *know* what I did!

ALICE: I know, but I thought—

ROMAN: God damn it! You called my wife! You don't know! You don't know what she believes! You don't know what I believe! Look. You and I happen to follow each other up here two years ago and we fucked. That's what we did. We fucked each other! I was leaving for Chicago in two days, so the truth is it was like a perfect send off. That's what it was for me. A send off. It's chilling I know, but it's the truth! I have no idea what it was for you, or what you were after, or thought you found, but all this talk about integrity, courage, being pushed and pulled together, it's just so incredibly infuriating to listen to you sputter! YOU CALLED MY WIFE! Who do you think you are!!!

ALICE: I know this is a scary time, but I didn't know—

ROMAN: No! This isn't scary! No! *(Roman smashes the alter.)* That's scary! *(Smashes it again.)* That's scary! Are you scared! *(Smashes.)* Scared yet? Come here. *(Pulls her into the wreckage and raises his hammer.)* This is scary! This is fear! This is losing your moral compass! This is what happens when you don't believe in anything! *(He releases her and walks away. A long silence. Cries softly.)* Oh God…

(Long silence.)

ALICE: *(Softly.)* …Roman…

ROMAN: *(Whispers.)* I'm sorry.

ALICE: I don't know what I was thinking.

ROMAN: I'm sorry I did that. I've never done something like that—

ALICE: I'm a fool, I am.

ROMAN: I wouldn't hurt you, I—

ALICE: No, God, I know. It's my fault—

ROMAN: I would never—

ALICE: —I'm just careless, I would never mean to—

ROMAN: —hurt someone. I just…

ALICE: —to cause you pain. I'm a fool.

ROMAN: I don't know what's wrong with me.

(Silence. Alice watches Roman.)

ALICE: God, what do you do when you see your whole life turn from hope, to just nothing.

ROMAN: That's not me. I'm not lost, I'm not…

(She begins to clean things up.)

ALICE: You? *(Laughs.)* I wasn't thinking of you.

(Beat.)

ROMAN: Alice…

(We hear the accordion and the fiddle as they ineptly make their way through the waltz. They stop and start again throughout the following. She continues to clean up.)

ALICE: In the last scene of André's film there's a moment when Galbraith, that's the man's name, returns to the place where he was going to build his observatory. A place like this. You know, he's been banished, shamed, branded a madman, everything's been taken from him, even his name, and then there's this image of him standing on this hilltop, in the middle of the night, and he throws his head back and starts to turn. Slowly at first, then faster, and he looks a little crazy, but he smiles and you wonder, is he content, or is he mad, or is he…It's just this perfect moment and you wonder, has he lost everything, or…There's this image, you know. No words.

(The musicians finally resolve. Fade to black.)

END OF PLAY

Degas, C'est Moi

BY DAVID IVES

THIS PLAY IS FOR MARTHA,
OF COURSE

THE AUTHOR

David Ives was born in Chicago and educated at Northwestern University and Yale School of Drama. He is probably best known for his evenings of one-act comedies, *All in the Timing* (1993) and *Mere Mortals* (1997). Among his other plays are *Ancient History, Don Juan in Chicago,* and *The Red Address.* In 1995 he received a Guggenheim Fellowship in playwriting. He lives in New York City.

ORIGINAL PRODUCTION

Degas, C'est Moi was presented as part of Marathon '96 at Ensemble Studio Theatre (Curt Dempster, Artistic Director) in New York City, on May 8, 1996. It was directed by Shirley Kaplan; the set design was by Mike Allan; the costume design was by David K. Mickelsen; the lighting design was by Greg MacPherson; the sound design was by Jeffrey Taylor; and the stage manager was Eileen Myers. The cast was as follows:

ED	Don Berman
DORIS	Susan Greenhill
MAN	Chris Lutkin
WOMAN	Ilene Kristen

Degas, C'est Moi was subsequently revised and presented as part of the evening titled *Mere Mortals,* which premiered at Primary Stages in New York (Casey Childs, Artistic Director) in May, 1998. It is that revised edition of the play which is published here.

CHARACTERS

ED
DORIS
MAN
WOMAN

Lights up on Ed, on a bed. Morning light.

ED: A stroke of genius. I decide to be Degas for a day. Edgar Degas. Why Degas? says a pesky little voice at the back of my head. Well why not Degas? Pourquoi pas Degas? Maybe the prismatic bars of color on my ceiling have inspired me.

(We see prismatic bars of color.)

ED: Maybe the creamy white light spreading on my walls has moved me.

(Creamy white light spreads on the wall.)

ED: Maybe it's all the cheap French wine I've been drinking. *(He finds a wine bottle in his bed.)* Anyway I don't have to explain myself. Yes! Today, I will be Edgar Degas!—Is it Edgar, or Edouard? Okay, so I don't know much about Degas. Let's see. Dead, French, impressionist painter of what, jockeys, ballerinas, flowers, that kinda thing. And okay granted, I'm not French, dead, or a painter of any kind. Not a lotta common ground. And yet, and yet—are Degas and I not united by our shared humanity? By our common need for love, coffee, deodorant?

(Doris enters.)

DORIS: Oh God, oh God, oh God. Have you seen my glasses?

ED: Doris breaks in on my inspiration.

DORIS: I can't find my glasses.

ED: Doris, I say to Doris, I'm going to be Degas today.

DORIS: He's gonna kill me if I'm late again.

ED: Doris doesn't see the brilliance of the idea.

DORIS: This is a tragedy.

ED: Doris—I am Degas!

DORIS: You're what?

ED: Is it Edgar or Edward? It's Edgar, isn't it.

DORIS: Don't forget the dry cleaning. *(Doris kisses him.)* 'Bye. *(Doris exits.)*

ED: Alas, poor Doris. Distracted by the banal. No matter. I start my day and brush my teeth as Degas. *(Ed produces a green toothbrush.)*

ED: Oh man. This is wonderful! In the bathroom, everything seems transfigured yet nothing has changed. The very porcelain pullulates with possibilities. Will you look at the lustre of that toilet? And the light on that green plastic! The bristles are disgusting, but the light is fantastic! *(French accent.)* Per'aps I weel paint you later.

(We hear the sound of shower running.)

ED: In the shower, it feels strange, lathering an immortal. What's even stranger, the immortal is lathering back. How did I become such a

genius? I, who flunked woodshop in high school? Was it my traumatic childhood? Did I have a traumatic childhood? There was Uncle Stosh's unfortunate party trick with the parakeet. Ouch. Well something must've happened. Because now I'm great. I'm brilliant. My name will live forever! *(He considers that a second.)* Whoo. Wow. This is too big for me to contemplate. I go out into the world with dry cleaning.
(He grabs some clothing as we hear city noises, car horns, etcetera.)

ED: O glorious polychromatic city! Gone the dreary daily deja vu. Today — Degas vu.
(A car driver enters at a run, holding a steering wheel, headed right for Ed. Loud car horn and screeching brakes heard as Ed dodges aside.)

DRIVER: Moron!

ED: Idiot!

DRIVER: Jerk! Watch where you're going!

ED: Do you know who you almost killed?

DRIVER: Yeah! An asshole! *(Driver exits.)*

ED: Another couple of inches and the world would've lost a hundred masterpieces.
(Dry Cleaner enters, writing on a pad.)

DRY CLEANER: Okay what's the dirt today?

ED: At the dry cleaners' I notice something strange...

DRY CLEANER: *(Taking the dry cleaning.)* One shirt, one skirt, one jacket.

ED: My dry cleaner acts exactly the same.

DRY CLEANER: You know you need some serious reweaving.

ED: Madame, how I would love to capture you in charcoal.

DRY CLEANER: My husband already caught me in puce. *(Tears a sheet off the pad.)* After five. *(The Dry Cleaner exits with the clothing.)*

ED: She gives not a flutter of recognition. Then on the corner, the newsguy tries to sell me my paper just like always.
(Newsguy enters.)

NEWSGUY: Daily Noose?

ED: Actually, have you got anything en francaise?

NEWSGUY: Let's see, I got Le Mot, Le Monde, Le Reve, Le Chat, La Chasse, L'Abime and Mademoiselle Boom Boom.

ED: I'll just take the News.

NEWSGUY: Change.
(He flips an invisible coin, which Ed "catches," then the Newsguy exits.)

ED: Still not a blink of recognition. Then as I head down Broadway, people pass me by without a second glance. Or even a first glance.

(People enter and pass him.)

ED: I might as well be invisible. I, Edgar Degas! And then I realize with a shock: it makes no difference to be Degas. To all these people, I could be anyone! And if I'm anyone—then who are all these people?

(More people pass him.)

ED: And yet…And yet maybe the other Degas walked this invisibly through Paris.

(We hear a French accordion.)

ED: Maybe he too was rudely bumped into by the bourgeoisie on the upper Left Bank…

(A Pedestrian bumps into him as a Worker enters carrying a crate loaded with cabbages.)

ED: Shouted at by workers at the Key Food de Montparnasse…

KEY FOOD WORKER: Watcha back, watcha back! *(Worker exits.)*

ED: Cursed by the less fortunate.

(Homeless person enters.)

HOMELESS PERSON: Fuck you. Fuck you.

ED: And you know, there's a kind of comfort in this.

HOMELESS PERSON: Fuck you.

ED: Completely anonymous, I'm free to appreciate the grey cloud of pigeons overhead…

(We hear the cooing of pigeons.)

ED: The impasto at Ray's Pizza…

PIZZA MAN: Pepperoni!

ED: The chiaroscuro of the M-Eleven bus.

(Loud motor of a city bus.)

ED: Nobody knows it, but I am walking down this street with a jewel cupped in my hands. The secret precious jewel of my talent.

(Unemployment Worker enters.)

UNEMPLOYMENT WORKER: Next!

ED: My delicious anonymity continues at Unemployment.

(A sign descends: "Unemployment Line Here.")

UNEMPLOYMENT WORKER: Sign your claim at the bottom, please.

ED: Do you notice the name I signed in the bottom right corner?

UNEMPLOYMENT WORKER: Edgar Day-hass. Edgar Deejis. Edgar Deggis. Edgar De Gas. Edgar De What?

ED: Edgar Degas. And—?

UNEMPLOYMENT WORKER: And—this name at the bottom does not match the name at the top of the form.

ED: No, no, no, no…

UNEMPLOYMENT WORKER: Are you not the same person as the person at the top of the form?

ED: I am a person at the top of my form. I am Edgar. Degas.

UNEMPLOYMENT WORKER: The dead French painter?

ED: The same.

UNEMPLOYMENT WORKER: Next!

(Unemployment Worker exits and the sign goes away.)

ED: Recalling my painterly interest in racetracks, I stop off at OTB.

(OTB Worker enters.)

OTB WORKER: Next!

ED: Ten francs on Windmill, s'il vous plait.

OTB WORKER: Oh mais oui, monsieur.

ED: Windmill—I say to him—because the jockey wears brilliant silks of crimson and gold. Windmill—I tell the man—because her sable flanks flash like lightning in the field. Windmill—I continue—because in form and moving she doth express an angel.

OTB WORKER: *(Handing over the betting slip.)* Windmill—

ED: —he says to me—

OTB WORKER: —always comes in last.

(Racing bell.)

ED: And Windmill does.

(Buzzer.)

ED: But who gives a shit? *(Tears up the betting slip.)* I'm Degas!

(OTB Worker exits. Ed looks around.)

ED: Oh—the library. Maybe I should look myself up.

(A sign descends: "Silence." A Librarian enters.)

LIBRARIAN: Shhhhhh!

ED: Excuse me. Have you got anything on Degas?

LIBRARIAN: Degas. You mean the crassly conservative counterfeminist patriarchal pedophile painter?

ED: No, I mean the colorist who chronicled his age and who continues to inspire through countless posters, postcards and T-shirts.

LIBRARIAN: Section D, aisle 2.

ED: Patriarchal pedoph…

LIBRARIAN: Quiet! *(Librarian exits.)*

ED: But who needs the carping of critics, the lies of biographers? I know who I am. Famished by creativity, I stop at Twin Donut.

(Two tables appear. A Young Woman sits at one, writing in a journal. Ed sits at the other.)

TWIN DONUT WORKER: *(Enters with a plate.)* Vanilla cruller!

ED: So there I am, scribbling a priceless doodle on my napkin when I notice someone staring at me.

(The Young Woman stops writing and looks at Ed.)

ED: A young woman writing in a journal. Has she recognized me? She smiles slightly. Yes. She knows I am Degas. Not only that.

(He looks again. The Young Woman starts writing.)

ED: She loves Degas. That one look has redeemed all my years of effort. My work has given meaning to someone's life. Should I seduce her? It would be traditional.

(A schmaltzy-romantic violin is heard.)

YOUNG WOMAN: *(Writing.)* "April six. Twin Donut. Just saw Edgar Degas two tables over. So he likes vanilla crullers too! Suddenly this day is glorious and memorable. Would love to lie in bed all afternoon and make l'amour with Degas…"

ED: But no. I'd only cast her off, break her heart. Not to mention what it would do to Doris.

YOUNG WOMAN: "Dwayne would kill me."

ED: But isn't it my duty as an artist to seduce this girl? Experience life to the fullest…?

YOUNG WOMAN: Adieu.

ED: Adieu.

(Young Woman exits.)

ED: Too late.

(Tables disappear. Afternoon light.)

ED: On Fifth Avenue, a mysterious figure passes me, leading a Doberman. Or vice versa.

(A figure in a raincoat, hat and sunglasses, holding a stiffened leash, as if a dog were on it, crosses.)

ED: It's somebody famous. But who? Kissinger? Woody Allen? Roseanne?

(Figure exits.)

ED: Whoa, whoa, whoa, just for a picosecond there, I forgot who I am! just for a moment—I seem to be nobody. The labor of hangingonto one's iden-tity!

(Empty picture frames descend and a Museum Guard enters.)

ED: At the museum I am simply amazed to find how much I accomplished— even without television.

(Degas self-portrait appears.)

ED: What's this... Ah. A self-portrait. Not a great likeness, maybe. But so full of...what?...feeling. I stare into my fathomless eyes.

(A Museum Goer stands beside him looking at the portrait.)

MUSEUM GOER: Mmm.

ED: Mmmmmmm.

MUSEUM GOER: Bit smudgy, isn't it?

ED: "Smudgy"?

MUSEUM GOER: This area in here.

ED: Yeah, but what about this area over here?

MUSEUM GOER: No, but look at this area here. This is smudge.

ED: Okay. So I had an off day.

MUSEUM GOER: An "off day"...?

ED: Not all my work was perfect.

MUSEUM GOER: Indeed. How could it be...? *(The Museum Goer slips away.)*

ED: Philistine. Probably headed for Van Gogh. To kneel in adoration at the sunflowers. I couldn't believe it, the day he started signing his paintings "Vincent." *We* called him "Vince." What a jerk.

(Degas's "Woman with Chrysanthemums" appears.)

ED: Ah yes. "Woman with Chrysanthemums." A personal favorite among my masterworks. God, when I remember that morning over a century ago...Can it be that long now? This was an empty canvas and I stood in front it paralyzed by its whiteness. Then I reached for my brush... *(Produces a paintbrush.)* ...and the picture crystallized. In a moment I saw it all. This pensive woman, oblivious of the transcenburst of color right at her shoulder. The natural exuberance of the flowers alongside her human sorrow. Yes. Yes! Our blindness to the beautiful! Our insensibility to the splendor right there within our reach!

MUSEUM GUARD: Step back, please.

ED: Excuse me?

MUSEUM GUARD: You have to step back, sir. You're too close to the painting.

ED: I'm too close to this painting...?

MUSEUM GUARD: Do you copy?

ED: No, I don't copy. I am an original!

MUSEUM GUARD: Sir?

ED: I step back.

(He does so, and the Guard exits.)

ED: But the glow of my exaltation stays with me all the way to the Akropolis Diner...

(A table. Doris enters.)

DORIS: Oh God, oh God.

ED: …where Doris meets me for dinner.

DORIS: What a day.

ED: What a fabulous day. Epic!

DORIS: Six hours of xeroxing.

ED: No, listen. Degas. Remember?

DORIS: Degas…?

ED: I've been Degas all day.

DORIS: The toilets erupted again. The women's room was like Vesuvius.

ED: I am Degas.

DORIS: They were going to fix those toilets last week.

ED: As Doris dilates on toilets, I begin to feel Degas slip away a little…

DORIS: Waiter!

ED: …like a second skin I'm shedding…

DORIS: Waiter!

ED: …leaving nothing behind.

DORIS: Where is that guy?

ED: Then I see a man at another table, staring at me. Looking at me with such pity. Such unalloyed human sympathy.

DORIS: At least I found my glasses.

ED: An then I realize.

DORIS: They were in my purse all the time.

ED: The man is Renoir.

DORIS: *(Holding up her glasses.)* See?

ED: By now, Degas is completely gone.

(Light changes to night light as Ed and Doris rise.)

ED: Doris and I walk home in silence.

(Doris exits. Lights darken to a single spot on Ed.)

ED: People say they have a voice inside their heads. The voice that tells themselves the story of their lives. Now I'm walking up the street, now I'm taking out my key, when did that streetlight burn out, is there a meaning to all this, who's that person coming down the stairs, now I'm putting my key in the door, now I do this, now I do that. The facts of our lives. Yes, I too have always had a voice like that in my head. But now, tonight, no one is listening. That presence that always listened in the back of my mind is no longer there, listening in. Nor is there a presence behind that presence listening in. Nor a presence behind that, nor behind that, nor behind that. All the way back to the back of my mind, no one is listening in. The story of my life is going on unwatched. Unheard. I am alone.

(The bed reappears.)

ED: I find myself upstairs, sprawled on the bed while Doris runs the bathwater. Degas is dust. All my glory, all my fame, all my achievements are utterly forgotten. Immortality? A cruel joke. The jewel I bore through the streets in the cup of my hands is gone, and my hands are empty. I have done nothing. Absolutely nothing.

(A light comes up on Doris, drying herself with a towel.)

ED: Then I find myself looking through the doorway into the bathroom and I see Doris standing naked with her foot up on the edge of the old lion-footed tub, drying herself. The overhead light is dim, but Doris is fluorescent—radiant—luminous—with pinks and lavenders and vermillions playing over her skin. The frayed towel she's wrapped in gleams like a rose. She turns and looks back at me and smiles.

(Doris turns and looks over her shoulder at Ed.)

DORIS: Bon soir, Degas.

ED: Degas…Who needs him?

(He holds his hand out to her across the intervening space, and she holds hers out to him.)

(Lights fade.)

END OF PLAY

Geliebteh

BY HOWARD KORDER

THE AUTHOR

Howard Korder was born in New York City in 1957, and graduated from the State University of New York at Binghamton. His first play, *Night Maneuver*, was produced in 1982 by the Floating Rep in New York City. *Episode 26* was presented Off-broadway by the Lamb's Theater in 1985. The Manhattan Punch Line produced *Life on Earth* in its 1985 One-Act Festival, and *Lip Service* the following year. Korder's *Fun,* directed by Jon Jory, premiered at Actors Theatre of Louisville's 1987 Humana Festival, and received the Heideman Award for Best One-Act Play. Its companion piece, *Nobody,* was selected for the 1987 O'Neill Playwrights Conference, where it won the HBO Writer's Award. Both plays were subsequently presented in New York at the Manhattan Punch Line, the American Repertory Theatre in Cambridge, among others.

Boys' Life was presented by Lincoln Center in 1988, directed by W.H. Macy and featuring the Atlantic Theatre Company, and received a nomination for a Pulitzer Prize. It is produced frequently at theatres around the world. The same year HBO broadcast Korder's television adaptation of *Lip Service,* which won a Cable Ace Award for Best Comedy Special.

Search and Destroy was commissioned by California's South Coast Repertory, premiering there in 1990 under the direction of David Chambers. It received the Los Angeles Theatre Critics' Award for best new play, and the Joseph Kesselring Prize from the National Arts Club. A production at Yale Repertory Theatre followed, and the play opened on Broadway at Circle in the Square in 1992. A critically acclaimed produciton of *Search and Destroy* opened at the Royal Court Theatre in London in May 1993 under the direction of Stephen Daldry. A film version, released in 1995, was produced by Martin Scorsese, and starred Griffin Dunne and Christopher Walken.

The Lights was produced at Lincoln Center Theatre in Fall 1993 under the direction of Mark Wing-Davey and received seven Drama Desk nominations and an Obie Award for Playwriting. It most recently was presented at the Royal Court Theatre in London.

Mr. Korder is the recipient of a 1996 Guggenheim Fellowship in Play Writing. Currently, he lives in New Mexico, where he is at work on a new play for South Coast Repertory.

ORIGINAL PRODUCTION

Geliebteh was originally produced at The Ensemble Studio Theatre, May 1996. It was directed by Matthew Penn with the following cast:

Woman . . . . Lynn Cohen

CHARACTER

WOMAN

Lights up on a Woman in her seventies.

WOMAN: Since you've asked me…

When I think of my father the first thing I remember is his hands. They were long and beautiful, thin tapered fingers, blue veins beneath the pale skin on the back. Musician's hands, you had to think. A violinist who would play with great feeling. But he wasn't musical. I never knew him to sing, or hum, or even whistle. Did he? Walking home from work, under the trees at Tompkins Square, a spring evening, perhaps his jacket slung over his shoulder, yes, I can imagine it, in such a circumstance a person might be expected to whistle. A moment of…release. A breeze stirs the leaves. A private moment on a warm spring evening in the city. Could it have happened? It's possible. Certainly it's possible.

He was a dressmaker. He worked in…oh, many places. Essex, Rivington, Eldridge…Ludlow Street. At first with his own machine. Not many know this now. But the piece workers, before they could be hired, they somehow had to buy their own sewing machines. Naturally you would think "how do I buy such a thing when I don't have a job?" There must be a story there. I never heard it. I never thought to learn. Only now, of course. Only now.

There were five seasons in our house. The fifth season was when my father didn't work. In that season, he would still be at home when I got ready to go to school. Sitting in the kitchen, fully dressed in vest and coat as who was not at that time, reading the paper with great methodicalness. I would keep out of his way. He had already been to minyan. Later he might occupy a bench in the park with some other men, similarly dressed. They had the look of people under doctor's orders, taking the air, waiting to feel better. Waiting for the season to change. In Yiddish they discussed deep matters. The Union…a socialist state…the Midrash…I don't know what they talked about. It was beyond me then. And now, how would I find out. That world is gone.

Once on my way home from school I heard a man call my name. I was seven, eight years old. I turned around, and here was my father with the other men all in dark heavy suits on their bench, smoking cigars, my father with a fat cigar like a millionaire. Come here, he said. Come over here. Well, you know how a child is. The thoughts that run through your head. What had I done wrong that he should be waiting for me here? To single me out in this public place? I went over. I stood before him. This is my daughter, he said to the men in English. In school she studies. Such a good one she is. His hand on my cheek gentle as a feather. Oh my heart raced. My God. My God.

Also in that time, which you don't see anymore, the funerals. Everyday it seemed the street had a procession, the mourners trailing behind a horse-drawn hearse. These were not Jewish ceremonies. The Italians, the Polish, weeping in the street, the widow howling at the top of her lungs, it sounds funny now, but at the time it frightened me. Into the kitchen I came crying, there were my parents, my mother by the stove, staring at the floor, my father at the table with his hand tight over his mouth. Without a word he leapt up and gave me such a crack across the head it knocked me down. My mother shrieked and ran to shield me. But my father just stood there. "Yes, that's how it is, all of you," he said. He grabbed his hat and rushed out, clumping down the four flights of stairs. Now my mother was crying, I was crying, the people outside in the funeral were crying. And my father, he returned after a few hours. I was in bed, the bed I shared with my sister, I heard him come in, I could feel him standing over me, the smell of him, of cigars and bay rum. But I pretended to go on sleeping, and after a while he went out.

Many years later I asked my mother what went on that night to make him so angry. But she didn't remember it at all. At the time it happened, she was maybe thirty-two years old. My father was thirty-seven. In a picture I have they are a handsome young couple, my mother with bright eyes and dark curly hair, such a lively face, my father thin and elegant. In their clothes rented from the photographer, they seem prosperous and confident. Between them I never saw a kiss, or a touch exchanged. But they must have loved each other. In some way there must have been love.

When the time came for me to work, my father got me a job through the union. I was a bobbin girl. I collected all the empty bobbins from the machines and spooled on new thread. There was never a moment's pause. Only once for a week were we in the same shop. When I could see him, across the rows of worktables, his head would be down, his fingers moving quickly around the needle, putting together dresses. He never waved to me, never looked up. He never said a word. Perhaps in that place, for a father and daughter, it wasn't right. Together we walked home, through some streets that weren't so nice, with goyishe men sitting on stoops, and they would say things as we passed that…at that time, I didn't understand. I was sixteen and so innocent. That kind of innocence today, it couldn't be. But then I knew nothing. Only my father, walking tight-lipped down this street, his hand under my elbow, he knew. He had to know. With his sense of dignity, his pride, it must have been difficult. A person like that, there are things they should never have to bear.

Eventually I passed the civil service exam. I was offered a job with the Health Department, and I could not wait to take it. I had been a bobbin girl, an edge trimmer, a presser, and I wanted no more of it. Now I would be uptown, I could go see a show after work, with girlfriends I could sit and have lunch. The test was not easy for me, I had to take it twice, and when I passed I felt I had achieved something. But all my father said was, "To go up there so far, every day you'll spend money for the train." It made me furious. I didn't want to *speak* to him. My brothers traveled to all the boroughs in their jobs, and at night, around the table, under the single lamp, they would ask my father for advice, about money, investing in property. He gave considered answers, he spoke to them as adults with serious issues to decide. But for me, enough to be a bobbin girl. He never asked about my job, the work I did, the things I had to learn. Never. When I said to him about City College, that I wanted to go, at night, to get a degree, you would think he'd forgotten English. There was no discussing the subject. No discussion at all. And then it was too late. I was twenty-six, twenty-seven, twenty-eight. Too late for such things.

What a relief for him when I met your father. I would be married, taken care of, a problem solved. And when you were born, the first son, a boy, such pride he had, he could not stop kissing you. He called you *knaydl,* which means a dumpling. Already then he was old. He was as old as I am now. Then your brothers, my own family, my own problems…So the things that were done, the things that weren't, there was no time to think about them anymore.

In the hospital, the last time he went in, a strange thing happened. It was not far from the end and his mind would wander. I was sitting next to the bed, suddenly in Yiddish he said, "Shut the door." I told him it was shut. "Now you'll listen. Not for another minute can I stand this," he said. "At the butcher you smile, the grocer, for all these men you have a kind word, and for your husband nothing. What do you do behind my back, you *kurveh?*" Which is…a terrible word. For a woman. A word you should never say. I didn't know what to think. Finally I said, "Poppa, it's Esther. I'm Esther." He looked at me for a long time and turned away.

Shortly afterwards he passed on. At the funeral, old men, tiny, bent over, strangers to me, they came up to say they knew him. They told me stories, about how he joked, he could have the whole room laughing, his generosity, once he gave a week's salary to the family of a man run down in the street, how he stood up to the boss about wages in the time before the union. They seemed to be talking about a different person. This man had my father's name, his face, his hands. I never met him. I never saw this man in my life.

The unveiling was a cold day. We didn't want to stay outside too long. The stone had both their names, well, you've seen it. My brothers left early, their wives were very impatient. So it was just Ruth and myself. We stopped for coffee after, somewhere off Northern Boulevard. Neither of us wanted to talk. After a while my sister said to me, "To him you were always the *geliebteh.*" Now for Ruth to speak Yiddish, it's unusual. She never learned it, from the start she only spoke English. She was the first. "What do you mean?" I said. "Why do you say this?" "Because I heard him. Because I know. One night at the table, you weren't there, momma was saying, I don't remember, something you didn't do you were supposed to, and poppa goes, 'Nothing against her. I don't want to hear. Esther, Esther is my *geliebt, geliebt kinder.*'"

And this word means, it means...

Ah, I was shaking. Just like that. My God. I could not take a breath. A grown woman and three sons of my own. I had a coffee in my hands, I saw the traffic outside on Northern Boulevard, but where I was...I don't know. I don't know. I was very far away. I was in the past. Did he say that? Could that have happened? Did my father think of me, did he see me in his mind as he sat there in the yellow light, long ago, so long ago now, and call me the beloved?

THE END

Love Like Fire

BY ROMULUS LINNEY

FOR LAURA CALLANAN

Love, like fire, can't last without moving,
or live without fear and hope.

Maxim 75
Duc de La Rochefoucauld

THE AUTHOR
Romulus Linney is the author of three novels, sixteen long and twenty short plays, staged throughout the United States and abroad. They include *The Sorrows of Frederick, Holy Ghosts, Childe Byron, Heathen Valley* and *"2".* He has won two Obie Awards, two National Critics Awards, three DramaLogue Awards, Fellowships from the NEA, Rockefeller and Guggenheim Foundations, and the Award in Literature from the American Academy and Institute of Arts and Letters, among others. He teaches playwrights in the Actors Studio MFA Program at the New School.

ORIGINAL PRODUCTION
Love Like Fire was originally produced at The Ensemble Studion Theatre, May 1996. It was directed by the author, assistant director was Robert Montgomery, with the following cast:

Mademoiselle/Princess.	Melinda Hamilton
Prince	Bill Cwikowski
Duke	Thomas Schall
King	Chris Ceraso
Chamberlain	John Martin Green

CHARACTERS
MADEMOISELLE, LATER PRINCESS

DUKE

PRINCE

KING

CHAMBERLAIN

PLACE
A French Court

TIME
Middle ages

from *The Princess of Cleves,* a novel by Madame de Lafayette

A beautiful carpet, with a simple, wooden bench at center. Music: Rameau: La Livri, from Pieces de Clavecin, 1741.

SCENE 1

Enter Prince, a distinguished man of 50, and Duke, a handsome man in his 20s. They wear tuxedos. Enter Mademoiselle, 20. She wears a beautiful modern dress and cloak. Enter Chamberlain. He wears a tuxedo with a scarlet jacket. He carries a mailed leather glove. All wait. Enter King, briskly, a vigorous, physical man in his forties, dressed in formal but festive dress. All kneel. Music ends.

KING: Mademoiselle.
(Mademoiselle rises, steps forward.)
KING: We mourn the death of your father. Live your life at Court.
(She bows her head, steps back.)
KING: Prince.
(The Prince rises, steps forward.)
KING: Your advice was effective. Congratulations.
(The prince bows his head, steps back. King holds out his hand. Chamberlain fits the mailed leather glove on it.)
KING: Duke.
(The Duke rises, steps forward.)
KING: You are ridiculous. *(King wiggles his hand in the glove.)* One year exile. Become a gentleman before you return.
(The Duke bows his head, steps back. King strips off glove, slaps it into the hands of the Chamberlain.)
KING: I'll use this. *(Exit King.)*
(Rameau's La Livri again. Exit Duke. Exit Chamberlain. Slow changes of light. Time passes. Prince and Mademoiselle sit on bench. La Livri ends.)

SCENE 2

PRINCE: Why won't you look at me?
MADEMOISELLE: *(Turning.)* But I will.
PRINCE: Not like that.
MADEMOISELLE: How?
PRINCE: What do you see when you look at me?

MADEMOISELLE: A friend.

PRINCE: You don't know what I'm talking about.

MADEMOISELLE: But I do.

PRINCE: Will you marry me?

MADEMOISELLE: Yes!

(She leans toward him. He stops her.)

PRINCE: For *me.*

MADEMOISELLE: Yes, for you.

PRINCE: Be sure.

MADEMOISELLE: I am! I blush when I see you!

PRINCE: Modesty!

MADEMOISELLE: Love!

PRINCE: No fever! No longing! What I feel for you, do you understand?

MADEMOISELLE: I can't feel what you tell me to!

PRINCE: Because you don't know what it is!

MADEMOISELLE: What can I say to that?

PRINCE: *(Smiling.)* I'm old, you're young. It's hopeless.

MADEMOISELLE: My mother and father were old when I was born. My mother
died. My father died. I have missed them. Yes, you are older than I am.
You are calm and wise, and good and strong. And I know you love me.
That is what I want.

*(The Prince holds out his hand to her. She takes it. He kisses her hand, then
her neck, then her mouth. She responds. La Livri.)*

SCENE 3

*Enter Chamberlain, with a chair. Enter Prince and Princess. Enter Duke,
King, and Prince, carrying a small object draped with a black velvet cloth.
King sits. Prince removes the cloth, revealing a small kaleidoscope. La Livri ends.*

PRINCE: Portrait of my wife.

KING: In a kaleidoscope. Delightful.

PRINCE: The artist had a reluctant subject.

KING: *(To Princess.)* Why?

PRINCESS: I did not think it worthwhile.

PRINCE: But I did.

KING: So do I. We accept your gift.

PRINCE: That is a great honor.

(The King holds the kaleidoscope out to the Duke.)

KING: Duke?
    (The Duke looks at it, hands it back.)
DUKE: Excellent. Convincing. Elegant.
KING: But?
DUKE: A little stiff.
KING: Why?
DUKE: There is a kind of life that cannot be captured. *(To Princess.)* In glass.
PRINCESS: It is a little stiff. So am I.
PRINCE: She is not!
PRINCESS: I didn't want it done at all, and now I don't want to look at it.
KING: Refreshing.
PRINCE: An angel.
PRINCESS: Who is a little stiff. The Duke is honest.
DUKE: I say what I feel.
KING: Everyone says what they feel, nobody what they really think.
    (Enter Chamberlain.)
CHAMBERLAIN: Majesty.
KING: Yes? *(The King hands the kaleidoscope to the Princess.)*
CHAMBERLAIN: On the jousting field, in practice with sword and mace, Chevalier de la Barre suffered a severed hand and broken arm. The arm must be amputated.
KING: The devil!
    (Exeunt King, Prince, Chamberlain, Duke. Princess sets the kaleidoscope and its velvet cloth on the bench. Duke returns. Pause. Princess and Duke stare at each other. Princess abruptly looks away.)
DUKE: You won't look at me.
    (She looks at him.)
DUKE: I am a man too often in love. I am a joke.
PRINCESS: Why is it so important to you?
DUKE: It is the best of life.
PRINCESS: Why?
DUKE: It is when I am most myself.
PRINCESS: No. To be in love all the time is to be someone else all the time.
DUKE: You are wrong.
PRINCESS: What an empty life you must have.
DUKE: It is not empty now.
PRINCESS: I'm glad.
DUKE: Is your life so satisfying?
PRINCESS: Yes.

DUKE: You may change your mind.

PRINCESS: I don't think so.

DUKE: Are you sure?

PRINCESS: I am.

> *(Duke looks at Princess, then goes to the kaleidoscope. He takes it from the bench, wraps it in its velvet cloth, puts it in his pocket.)*

PRINCESS: What are you doing?

DUKE: Stealing your portrait. Do I give it up, or, because I must have something of you, do I keep it? Decide.

> *(Enter Prince.)*

PRINCE: Terrible. The Chevalier de la Barre, sword drawn, was so eager to strike, he hit his own wrist. The hand came clean off. He did it to himself. *(The Prince looks for the portrait.)* Madame? *(Pause.)* My portrait? *(Prince looks from Princess to Duke.)*

DUKE: The Princess and I walked to the end of the gallery. When we came back, it was gone. We thought you had returned and taken it.

> *(Pause. Prince looks at Princess.)*

PRINCE: Really?

> *(Pause.)*

PRINCESS: Yes.

> *(La Livri. Exeunt Princess, Prince, Duke.)*

SCENE 4

> *Enter King. He sits on the bench. Enter Princess. She kneels before King. La Livri ends.*

KING: You don't like it here.

PRINCESS: I am trying.

KING: If you live at Court, you fall in love. It wouldn't happen to you?

PRINCESS: *(A whisper.)* I didn't think so.

KING: Now you know. It won't hurt long. We have no more say in the length of our love affairs than we do in the length of our lives. But when they burn, they burn. Yes?

PRINCESS: (Whisper.) Yes.

KING: Sit by me.

> *(She does.)*

KING: The Queen is giving birth, in our barbaric fashion. Do you know why it must take place in a bedroom full of people?

PRINCESS: No, Majesty.

KING: To keep someone from replacing our child with theirs and at my death claiming the throne. It has happened. Now, why am I here, with you?

PRINCESS: I don't know.

KING: Everything is custom. At the birth King is to be with another woman, preferably one of spotless reputation. That is one custom. There is another. You are in love with the Duke.

PRINCESS: Oh!

KING: You thought I couldn't tell?

PRINCESS: Yes.

KING: I will even tell you why. You find yourself loving him, not only because HE loves YOU, but because HE sees that YOU love HIM. What? You, in love with the most promiscuous man in France? Impossible. And you know the Duke will not expose his knowledge of your enslavement. Safety. But wait, you realize the King saw it. Danger. And if he can, dear God, who ELSE can? Threats. You? Wanting a man who may love you and who may not? Panic. Who might be playing with SOMEONE ELSE? Terror! While you surrender YOURSELF to HIM? AH!! Nothing matters now! Plague, disease, death, you loathe him, hate him, fear him, love him! Passion pulls open your white legs. He will shove himself inside you. You will deny him nothing. *(Pause.)* Then everything. Then nothing. Then everything, or embrace life in a convent. Love, like fire, can't last without moving, or live without fear and hope.

(Enter Chamberlain.)

CHAMBERLAIN: Majesty.

KING: Yes?

CHAMBERLAIN: One hour ago, the Queen cried out. She went quickly into labor. She was delivered of a stillborn child.

KING: Thank you.

(Exit Chamberlain.)

KING: Then Passion leaves us, with screaming lovers and dead babies. *(King touches Princess gently on the cheek.)* Leave this court. Make your husband take you away. Anything will be better than a humiliation he cannot endure, and a wretchedness you cannot imagine.

(La Livri. Exit King.)

SCENE 5

Enter Prince. Music ends.

PRINCE: The country?

PRINCESS: I am very tired.

PRINCE: We belong at Court.

PRINCESS: I want to be alone with you!

PRINCE: Why alone, with me or without me? *(Pause.)* Well?

PRINCESS: I am afraid.

PRINCE: Of what?

PRINCESS: Of myself.

PRINCE: What does that mean?

PRINCESS: I must not make mistakes a woman can make. I would die.
(Pause. The Prince nods.)

PRINCE: You are behaving perfectly. Who is he?
(She shakes her head.)

PRINCE: I know you are faithful to me. But, who is he?

PRINCESS: That isn't important.

PRINCE: Madame.

PRINCESS: How I avoid him is important.

PRINCE: *Madame.*

PRINCESS: Help me!

PRINCE: Madame!!

PRINCESS: Someone at Court. But a friend.

PRINCE: Friendship for a husband stops no one from making love to a wife.
It encourages it. I am not angry. You have done exactly right. But tell me
what I must know.

PRINCESS: No. It would have been easier to tell you nothing.

PRINCE: And leave me?

PRINCESS: I would never do that.

PRINCE: This is the way you looked the day your portrait was stolen. You gave
it away.

PRINCESS: I did not!

PRINCE: To the Duke!

PRINCESS: No!

PRINCE: Are you lovers yet?

PRINCESS: No.

PRINCE: I believe you.

PRINCESS: Would I do such a thing to you?

PRINCE: With opportunity, you *might*. *(Pause.)* What has he done to you?

PRINCESS: Don't make me tell you what fills me with shame.

PRINCE: Yes, don't answer.

PRINCESS: Then may we leave the Court?

PRINCE: More than ever, we must stay. I trust you and I believe in our marriage.

(La Livri. They part, and move to separate sides of the stage.)

SCENE 6

All onstage.

CHAMBERLAIN: On the 15th of June, his Majesty, together with the Princes Albert d'Este, Marechal de Saint-Andre; Francois de Lorraine, Chevalier de Guise; and Jacques de Savoie, Duke de Nemours, will hold an open tournament of horse and lance against all who qualify to do combat with them. The success and brilliance of this celebration is from this day the first concern of the Court.

KING: I will be with you, Prince, as I enter the lists. The Queen shall be attended by you, Princess, and by you, Duke. Rehearsals for this festival begin now. Prince, to me. Duke, conduct Madame to the Queen.

(Music. Exit King, Prince and Chamberlain. Duke goes to Princess, holds up his hand, and she must place hers upon it.)

PRINCESS: For God's sake!

DUKE: The King has put us together.

PRINCESS: Yes!

DUKE: I will not take advantage of it.

PRINCESS: Oh! Won't you?

(Music. Exit Duke.)

SCENE 7

Enter Prince. He sits. Princess touches him.

PRINCESS: You are freezing.

PRINCE: You have succeeded in your amazing designs. The King makes you the first companion of the Duke. The Court is laughing at me, the King loudest of all! What more do you want?

PRINCESS: Do you have a fever?

PRINCE: A chill. From watching my wife adore the most trivial man at Court, and watching the King give you to him! Did you ask him to?

PRINCESS: DO you have a fever?

PRINCE: Yes!

PRINCESS: Then I forgive you for thinking I could be given away to anyone. I expected you to be reasonable.

PRINCE: Reasonable? Me?

PRINCESS: I have been as strict with myself as a jailor with a key! I have done nothing behind your back I would not do to your face.

PRINCE: I have heard that all my life. I never expected to hear it from you. Where do you want me, while you spend your nights with him?

PRINCESS: With me!!

PRINCE: Then tell me he did not teach you what you did not know, how to love him.

(She bows her head.)

PRINCE: Do you know, now, when I asked you to marry me, what I wanted you to feel?

PRINCESS: Yes.

PRINCE: Now, you love! A man you can't resist!

PRINCESS: But I have resisted him! You must not believe these hateful things! The King told me I should leave the Court. You would not let me. So the King thinks I want to stay, and puts me where he thinks I want to be! That is your fault, not mine!

PRINCE: It's where you DO want to be!!

PRINCESS: I will go back to the King! I will protest his treatment of a woman who has done nothing wrong!

PRINCE: If you talk like that, he will disgrace us both.

PRINCESS: Let him! Anything is better than this! I will go to the King!

(Enter Chamberlain.)

CHAMBERLAIN: Though the day's preparations were over, the King decided to break one more lance before supper. He called for the Duke de Nemours to ride against him. They fought, their lances were shattered, and a dart of wood flew into the eyepiece of the King's helmet. He fell from his horse. The Duke de Nemours held him in his arms. The King forgave his opponent, as the splinter moved into his brain and killed him. The King is dead. The Queen is Regent of France.

(Exit Chamberlain.)

PRINCE: Who will protect you now? Not the King. The man you are in love with has just had the good fortune to kill him. As for me, to live with the woman I love while she loves someone else defiles the deepest feelings I have ever had. We won't see each other again.

PRINCESS: I did not betray you.

(Pause. Prince stares at Princess.)

PRINCE: You may be telling the truth. If so, wait a few years, you will both be free, and both completely innocent. And that is the sharpest of all the knives you have buried in my heart!

PRINCESS: Don't leave me.

PRINCE: I trust you will not completely forget our marriage. I believe you always wanted to feel for me what you had to feel for him.

(Exit Prince. La Livri.)

SCENE 8

Enter Duke, pacing back and forth. Enter Chamberlain.

CHAMBERLAIN: The Prince of Cleves, with firmness of spirit, died of a fever contracted as a loyal servant of our late King. His widow has closed the doors of her chambers and will receive no one. You are wasting your time.

(Exit Chamberlain. The Duke paces. Enter Chamberlain.)

CHAMBERLAIN: The Princess will not see you.

(Exit Chamberlain. The Duke paces. Enter Chamberlain.)

CHAMBERLAIN: No.

(Exit Chamberlain. The Duke paces. Enter Chamberlain.)

CHAMBERLAIN: Never.

(Enter Princess, in a black cloak. Exit Chamberlain.)

PRINCESS: Yes?

DUKE: I waited for your mourning to end. Allow me to talk to you.

PRINCESS: I will not allow you anything.

DUKE: I am behaving as well as I can.

PRINCESS: You are.

DUKE: Then stop me from loving you.

(Princess smiles at him.)

PRINCESS: How? You swim in love, like a fish in the sea. You have loved before and will again, over and over, all your life.

DUKE: I will never love anyone but you!

(Pause.)

PRINCESS: No? *(She sits on a bench.)* On my wedding night, my husband in my arms, I saw your face. It was the face of a fool. But in its mouth, it held the key to my body.

DUKE: And now we are free.

PRINCESS: Free?

DUKE: Yes!

PRINCESS: We destroyed my husband.

DUKE: Your husband died of pneumonia.

PRINCESS: Of pride and age. Shame and humiliation and disgust. With your sword through his heart.

DUKE: I did nothing to him!

PRINCESS: And the King?

DUKE: I beg your pardon?

PRINCESS: He's dead, too. You killed him, too.

DUKE: A splinter from a lance, no bigger than this, killed him. It was an accident witnessed by four hundred people. What awful things are you thinking now?

PRINCESS: The worst. The King died from love of his sword. My husband died from love of his wife. Love kills.

DUKE: What is this now, Princess, you are putting between us?

PRINCESS: For one time in my life I will let you see what I feel. You are free. I am free. We love each other. Nothing can stop us from honorably spending the rest of our lives together. But the only man who could love me forever was my husband. And he did that only because I could not love him. Love, like fire.

DUKE: We have done nothing wrong!

PRINCESS: We have done everything wrong!

DUKE: We are blameless!

PRINCESS: Are we? Then I challenge you! Forever and ever, Duke! Can you swear you will love me and no one else as long as you live?

(He does not answer.)

PRINCESS: Thank you.

(She turns to go. Arms outspread, he stops her.)

DUKE: But we love each other now! That is enough!

PRINCESS: It isn't.

DUKE: It has to be!

PRINCESS: It doesn't.

DUKE: LOOK AT ME!

PRINCESS: Your love looks like hate.

DUKE: What will you do?

PRINCESS: Escape!

DUKE: You can't escape from life!

PRINCESS: Of course I can!

DUKE: Leave the Court?

PRINCESS: Yes!

DUKE: Bury yourself?

PRINCESS: Yes!

DUKE: Where?

PRINCESS: With women!

DUKE: What women?

PRINCESS: You'll see!

DUKE: I will stand at your door and wait for you!

PRINCESS: It will be a very thick door!

DUKE: The church?

PRINCESS: Of course.

DUKE: The *convent?*

PRINCESS: Of course.

DUKE: You?

PRINCESS: I will marry a god I doubt exists. Embrace a faith I do not believe. My life, I leave behind, as a story for you to tell your women, proof of a love I will always have for you. *(She smiles, and bows her head.)*
(Music. The Duke reaches out to her, stops, bows, and leaves her. Light fades on the Princess, looking after him. Music ends.)

THE END

Elegy for a Lady

BY ARTHUR MILLER

ORIGINAL PRODUCTION

Elegy for a Lady was originally produced in tandem with *Some Kind of Love Story* at Long Wharf Theatre, New Haven, Connecticut, November 1982 under the omnibus title of *2 by AM*. It was directed by the author, with the following cast appearing in both plays:

Man .... Charles Cioffi
Proprietress .... Christine Lahti

The British premiere of *Two-Way Mirror (Elegy for a Lady and Some Kind of Love Story)* was at the Young Vic, London, in January 1989. The production was directed by David Thacker and starred Helen Mirren and Bob Peck.

Elegy for a Lady was produced at The Ensemble Studio Theatre, May 1996. It was directed by Curt Dempster with Christine Haag and James Murtagh.

CHARACTERS

MAN
PROPRIETRESS

The Man appears in a single beam of light, facing the audience. He is hatless, dressed in a well-fitted overcoat and tweed suit. He stares as though lost in thought, slightly bent forward, perhaps to concentrate better. He is deep into himself, unaware for the moment of his surroundings. Light rises behind him, gradually dawning across the stage, reveals aspects of what slowly turns out to be a boutique. The shop consists of its elements without the walls, the fragments seeming to be suspended in space. A sweater is draped over a bust, a necklace on another bust, a garter on an upturned plastic thigh, a watch on an upturned arm, a knitted cap and muffler on a plastic head. Some of these stand on elements of the counter-shape, others seem to hang in air. As the light rises to normal level the Man moves into the boutique. And now, among the displays a Woman is discovered standing motionless, looking off at an angle in passive thought. She is wearing a white silk blouse and a light beige skirt and high heeled shoes. The Man moves from object to object and pauses also to look into the display case in the counter where jewelry is kept. As he nears her, he halts, staring into her profile.

MAN: Can you help me?

PROPRIETRESS: *(Turns now to look into his eyes.)* Yes?

MAN: Do you have anything for a dying woman?

PROPRIETRESS: *(She waits a moment for him to continue and then looks about, trying to imagine.)* Well, let me see...
(He waits another instant, then resumes his search, examining a pair of gloves, a blouse.)

PROPRIETRESS: May I ask you if...? *(She breaks off when he does not respond or turn to her. Finally he does.)*

MAN: Excuse me?

PROPRIETRESS: I was just wondering if you meant that she was actually...

MAN: By the end of the month or so. Apparently.

PROPRIETRESS: *(Seeking hope.)* ...But it isn't sure.

MAN: I think *she's* sure. But I haven't talked to any doctors or anything like that...

PROPRIETRESS: And it's...?

MAN: *(Cutting in.)* So it seems, yes.

PROPRIETRESS: *(With helpless personal involvement.)* Ah.

MAN: *(Forcing out the words.)* ...I assume you were going to say cancer.

PROPRIETRESS: *(She nods with a slight inhale of air. Now she glances around at her stock with a new sense of urgency.)*

MAN: I started to send flowers, but flowers seem so...funereal.

PROPRIETRESS: Not necessarily. Some spring flowers?

MAN: What's a spring flower?—daisies?

PROPRIETRESS: Or daffodils. There's a shop two blocks down—Faynton's

MAN: *(Considers.)* I passed there twice. But I couldn't decide if it should be a bunch of flowers or a plant.

PROPRIETRESS: Well, either would be…

MAN: Except that a bunch would fade, wouldn't they?—in a few days?

PROPRIETRESS: But a plant would last. For years, sometimes.

MAN: But there's a suggestion of irony in that. Isn't there?

PROPRIETRESS: *(Thinks.)* Cut flowers, then.

MAN: They don't last at all, though, and she'd have to watch them withering away every morning…

PROPRIETRESS: Yes.

(Slight pause. He resumes looking at things, handles a bracelet.)

(Half asking.) She is not an older woman.

MAN: She just turned thirty…a couple of months ago.

PROPRIETRESS: *(She inhales sharply.)*

MAN: I've never really bought her anything. It struck me this afternoon. Nothing at all.

PROPRIETRESS: *(Delicately.)* You've known each other very…

MAN: *(Grieving.)* That's always hard to remember exactly. I can never figure out whether we met two winters ago or three. *(A little laugh which she joins.)* —She never can either…but we've never been able to stay on the subject long enough…in fact, on any subject—Except one.

(Proprietress laughs softly and he joins her for an instant.)

I'm married.

PROPRIETRESS: *(Nods.)* Yes.

MAN: And a lot older, of course.

PROPRIETRESS: Oh, Well that's not always a… *(Does not finish.)*

MAN: …No, but it is in most cases. *(He glances around again.)* I tried to think of a book. But after all the reading I've done nothing occurs to me.

PROPRIETRESS: She is not religious.

MAN: No—Although we never talked about religion. I don't know whether to try to concentrate her mind or distract it. Everything I can think to send her seems ironical; every book seems either too sad or too comical; I can't think of anything that won't increase the pain of it.

PROPRIETRESS: Perhaps you're being too tender. Nothing you could send would be as terrible as what she knows.

(He considers this, nods slightly.)

PROPRIETRESS: People do make a kind of peace with it.

MAN: No; I think in her case the alarm never stops ringing; living is all she ever thought about.—She won't answer the phone anymore. She doesn't return my calls for days, a week sometimes. I think, well, maybe she wants me—you know—to disappear, but then she does call back and always makes an excuse for not having called earlier. And she seems so desperate for me to believe her that I forget my resentment and I try to offer to help again and she backs away again...and I end up not seeing her for weeks again. *(Slight pause.)* I even wonder sometimes if she's simply trying to tell me there's somebody else. I can't figure out her signal.

PROPRIETRESS: Yes. But then again it might simply be that she...

MAN: That's right...

PROPRIETRESS: ...Finds it unbearable to be cheated of someone she loves...

MAN: I'm so glad to hear you say that!—it's possible... *(With relief, deeper intimacy.)* Sometimes, you know, we're on the phone and suddenly she excuses herself—and there's silence for a whole minute or two. And then she comes back on with a fresh and forward-looking attitude and her voice clear. But a couple of times she's cut out a split second too late, and I hear the rush of sobbing before she can clap her hand to the receiver. And it just burns my mind—and then when she comes back on so optimistically I'm in a terrible conflict; should I insist on talking about the reality, or should I pretend to sort of swim along beside her?

PROPRIETRESS: She's in a hospital.

MAN: Not yet.—Although, frankly, I'm not really sure. She's never home anymore, I know that. Unless she's stopped answering her phone altogether.—Even before this happened she would do that; but she's on the phone practically all day in her work so its understandable. Not that I'm ruling out that she might have been staying elsewhere occasionally.— But of course I've no right to make any demands on her. Or even ask any questions.—What does this sound like to you?

PROPRIETRESS: It sounds like you'd simply like to thank her.

MAN: *(With a slight surprise.)* Say! That's exactly right, yes!...I'd simply like to thank her. I'm so glad it sounds that way.

PROPRIETRESS: Well...why not just *do* that?

MAN: *(Anguished.)* But how can I without implying that she's coming to the end...? *(Breaks off.)*

PROPRIETRESS: But she's *said* she's...?

MAN: Not really in so many words; she just...as I told you...breaks up on the phone or...

PROPRIETRESS: *(With anguish now.)* Then why are you so sure she's…?

MAN: Because they're evidently operating on her in about ten days. And she won't tell me which hospital.

PROPRIETRESS: …When you say "evidently"…

MAN: Well, I know she's had this growth, and there was pain for awhile— about last summer—but then it passed and she was told it was almost certainly benign. But… *(He goes silent; stares at Proprietress.)* Amazing.

PROPRIETRESS: Yes?

MAN: I've never mentioned her at all to anyone. And she has never let on about me. I know that…and we have close mutual friends who have no idea. And here I walk in and tell you everything, as though… *(From an engaging chuckle the breath seems to suddenly go out of him and he sits weakly on a stool, struggling against helplessness.)*

PROPRIETRESS: Yes?

(He makes an attempt to resume looking around the store but it fails.)

PROPRIETRESS: When you passed here earlier today…

MAN: *(With great relief.)* Yes, that's right, I remember that! You saw me then…

PROPRIETRESS: You stared at the window for a very long time.

MAN: I was trying to think of something for her.

PROPRIETRESS: Yes, I could see you imagining; it moved me deeply—for her sake.

MAN: It's amazing how absolutely nothing is right. I've been all over this part of town. But every single thing makes some kind of statement that is simply…not right.

PROPRIETRESS: I'm sure you're going to think of something.

MAN: I hope so!

PROPRIETRESS: Oh I'm sure!

MAN: It's partly, I think, that I don't know what I want to say because I'm not sure what I have a right to say—I mean someone my age ought to be past these feelings.— *(With sudden revulsion.)* I go on as though there's all the time in the world…! *(He stands, quickened, looking at the goods again.)* That kerchief is beautiful.

PROPRIETRESS: It's silk. Paris. *(She unfurls it for him.)*

MAN: Lovely. How would you wear it?

PROPRIETRESS: Any way. Like this… *(She drapes it over her shoulders.)*

MAN: Hm.

PROPRIETRESS: Or even as a bandanna. *(She wraps it over her hair.)*

MAN: But she wouldn't do that indoors.

PROPRIETRESS: Well…she *could*.

MAN: No. I'm afraid it could taunt her.

PROPRIETRESS: *(Putting it back on her shoulders.)* Well, then—in bed, like this.

MAN: *(Tempted.)* It is the right shade.—You have her coloring, you know;—I can't get over it, walking in off the street like this and blabbing away.

PROPRIETRESS: A thing like that builds up: you never know who you'll suddenly be telling it to.

MAN: Except that you have a look in your eye.

PROPRIETRESS: *(Smiling.)* What kind of look?

MAN: *(Returns her smile.)* You're seeing me. *(Of the scarf, definitely now.)* That isn't right.

(She slips it off. He moves, looking about.)

MAN: ...I think it's also that you're just about her age.

PROPRIETRESS: Why would that matter?

MAN: Someone older usually forgets what thirty was really like.

PROPRIETRESS: But you remember?

MAN: I didn't used to—thirty is far back down the road for me; but when I'm with her it all flows back at the touch of her skin. I feel like a Hindu recalling a former life.

PROPRIETRESS: And what is thirty like?

MAN: Thirty is an emergency. Thirty is the top of the ridge from where you can see down both sides—the sun and the shadow, your youth and your dying in the same glance. It's the last year to believe that your life can radically change anymore. And now she's caught on that ridge, unable to move.—God... *(A surge of anguish.)* ...how *pleased* with herself she'd gotten lately!—her ambitions and plans really working out... *(With a half-proud, half embarrassed grin.)* although tough too—she can snap your head back with a harsh truth, sometimes. But I don't mind, because all it is is her wide-open desire to live and win. *(He glances around at the objects.)* So it's hard to think of something that won't suggest the end of all that...and those eyes closing.

PROPRIETRESS: I have a kind of warm negligee. That one up there.

MAN: *(Looks up, studies it for a moment.)* But that might look to her like something after you've had a baby.

PROPRIETRESS: Not necessarily.

MAN: Yes. Like when they stroll around the hospital corridors afterward...If she's very sick she'd have to be in a hospital gown, wouldn't she?

PROPRIETRESS: *(Sharply, like a personal rebellion.)* But *everybody* doesn't die of it! Not *every* case!

MAN: *(Explosively.)* But she weeps on the phone! I heard it!

PROPRIETRESS: *(A personal outcry.)* Well the thought of disfigurement is terrible, isn't it? *(She turns away, pressing her abdomen. Pause.)* You ought to write, and simply thank her.

MAN: *(Asking…)* But that *has* to sound like a goodbye!

PROPRIETRESS: You sound as though you never had a single intimate talk!

MAN: Oh yes, but not about…negative things, somehow.

PROPRIETRESS: You met only for pleasure.

MAN: Yes. But it was also that we both knew there was nowhere it could go. Not at my age. So things tend to float pretty much on the surface…

PROPRIETRESS: *(Smiling.)* Still, the point does come…

MAN: Surprisingly, yes…

PROPRIETRESS: When it begins to be an effort to keep it uncommitted…

MAN: Yes, there's a kind of contradiction…

PROPRIETRESS: —To care and simultaneously not-care…

MAN: You can't find a breakthrough—it's like a fish falling in love with the sun; once he breaks water he can't breathe!—So maybe the whole thing really doesn't amount to anything very much.

(Pause.)

PROPRIETRESS: *(She re-folds a sweater he had opened up.)* But you don't always look like this, do you?

MAN: How?

PROPRIETRESS: In pain.

MAN: I guess I'm still unable to understand what she means to me.—I've never felt this way about a death. Even my mother's and father's…there has always been some unwelcome, tiny feeling of release; an obligation removed. But in her case, I feel I'm being pulled under myself and suffocated.

(Proprietress takes a deeper breath of air and runs a hand down her neck.) What else do you have that might…? *(He halts as he starts once again to look around at the merchandise.)* …Wait! I know—a bed jacket! That's the kind of neutral—healthy people wear them too!

PROPRIETRESS: I haven't any.

MAN: Nothing at all?

PROPRIETRESS: You might try the department stores.

MAN: *(Greatly relieved.)* I will. I think that's what I want. A bed jacket doesn't necessarily say anything, you see?

PROPRIETRESS: That's true, there is something non-committal about a bed jacket. Try Saks.

MAN: Yes. Thanks very much.—I never dreamed I'd have such a conversation!

(Starts to button up. With embarrassment.) It really amazes me…coming in here like this…

PROPRIETRESS: I have an electric kettle if you'd care for a cup of tea.

MAN: …Thanks, I wouldn't mind, thanks very much…I simply can't get over it,…I had no idea all this was in me.

(She goes behind the counter, throws a switch; he sits at the counter again.)

MAN: Are you the owner here? *(He opens his coat again.)*

PROPRIETRESS: *(Nods affirmatively, then…)* You know, it may be a case of a woman who's simply terrified of an operation, that's all.—I'm that way.

MAN: *(Thinks, trying to visualize—then…)* No, I think it would take a lot more to panic her like this. She's not an hysterical person, except once a month for a few hours, maybe.

PROPRIETRESS: She tends to objectify her situation.

MAN: That's it.

PROPRIETRESS: Sees herself.

MAN: Yes.

PROPRIETRESS: From a distance.

MAN: Yes, she has guts; really cool nerve right up to the moment she flies to pieces.

PROPRIETRESS: She's had to control because she's alone.

MAN: Yes; so something like this must be like opening a shower curtain and a wild animal jumps out.

PROPRIETRESS: She was never married.

MAN: Never. *(Begins to stare off and smile.)*

PROPRIETRESS: Something about her couldn't be.—Unless to you?

MAN: *(Joyfully.)* She has a marvelous, throaty, almost vulgar laugh; it can bend her forward and she even slaps her thigh like a hick comedian…

(Proprietress begins laughing.)

MAN: …and gets so helpless she hangs on my arm and nearly pulls me down to the sidewalk.

(Proprietress laughs more deeply.)

MAN: One time at one of those very tiny cafe tables we both exploded laughing at the same instant, and our heads shot forward just as the waiter was lowering my omelet between us…

(She bursts out laughing and slaps her thigh. He sees this and his smile remains. The tea kettle whistles behind the counter.)

PROPRIETRESS: Milk or lemon?

(He watches her a moment, smiling.)

Lemon?

MAN: Lemon, yes.

(*She goes and pours tea. The Man, with a new anticipatory excitement.*)
You're not busy?

PROPRIETRESS: After Christmas it all dies for a few days. (*Hands him a cup.*)

MAN: It's more like somebody's home in here.

PROPRIETRESS: I try to sell only what I'd conceivably want for myself, yes.

MAN: You're successful.

PROPRIETRESS: In a way. (*Confessing.*) …I am, I guess.—Very, in fact.

MAN: But a baby would be better.

PROPRIETRESS: (*A flash of resentment, but then truth.*) …Sometimes. (*Hesitates.*) Often, actually. (*Looks around at the shop.*) It's all simply numbers, figures. Something appalling about business, something totally pointless—like emptying a pail and filling it again every day.—Why?— Do I look unhappy?

MAN: You look like you'd found yourself…for the fiftieth time and would love to throw yourself away again.

PROPRIETRESS: You try to avoid hurting people.

MAN: Yes, but it can't be helped sometimes. I've done it.

PROPRIETRESS: No wonder she loves you.

MAN: I'm not so sure. I really don't know anymore.

PROPRIETRESS: Oh, it must be true.

MAN: Why?

PROPRIETRESS: It would be so easy.

MAN: But I'm so old.

PROPRIETRESS: No.

MAN: I'm not sure I want her to. I warned her not to, soon after we started. I said there was no future in it. I said that these things are usually a case of loving yourself and wanting someone else to confirm it, that's all. I said all the blunt and ugly things I could think of.

PROPRIETRESS: And it didn't matter at all.

(*Slight pause.*)

MAN: It didn't?

PROPRIETRESS: (*With a hard truthfulness.*) Of course it mattered—what you said made her stamp on her feelings, and hold part of herself in reserve. It even humiliated her a little.

MAN: (*In defense.*) But her independence means more to her than any relationship, I think.

PROPRIETRESS: How do you know?—You were the one who ordered her not to love you…

MAN: Yes. *(Evading her eyes.)* But there's no tragic error, necessarily—I don't think she wanted to love anyone. In fact, I don't think either of us said or did anything we badly regret—it's Nature that made the mistake; that I should be so much older, and so perfectly healthy and she so young and sick.

PROPRIETRESS: *(Unnerved, an outburst.)* Why do you go on assuming it has to be the end!

(He looks at her with surprise.)

Thousands of people survive these things. And why couldn't you ask her what exactly it was?

MAN: I couldn't bear to make her say it.

PROPRIETRESS: Then all she's actually said was that an operation…?

MAN: No. Just that the 28th of the month was the big day.

PROPRIETRESS: *(Almost victoriously.)* Well that could mean almost anything.

MAN: *(In anguish.)* Then why doesn't she let me come and see her!

PROPRIETRESS: *(Frantically.)* Because she doesn't want to load her troubles onto you!

MAN: I've thought of that.

PROPRIETRESS: Of course. It's a matter of pride. Even before this happened, I'm sure she never encouraged you to just drop in, for instance—did she?

MAN: Oh no. On the contrary.

PROPRIETRESS: Of course not! She wanted her hair to be done and be dressed in something you'd like her in…

MAN: Oh, insisted on that, yes.

PROPRIETRESS: Then you can hardly expect her to invite you to see her in a hospital!

(Slight pause.)

MAN: Then it *is* all pretty superficial, isn't it.

PROPRIETRESS: Why!—it could be the most important thing in her entire life.

MAN: *(Pause. Shakes his head.)* No. Important—but not the most important. Because neither of us have burned our bridges. As how could we?—If only because of my age?

PROPRIETRESS: Why do you go on about your age? That's only an excuse to escape with.

MAN: *(Smiles.)* But it's the only one I've got, dear.—But what ever age I was, she wouldn't be good to be married to.

PROPRIETRESS: *(Hurt, almost alarmed.)* How can you say that!

MAN: What's wrong in saying it? She's still ambitious for herself, she still needs risks, accomplishments, new expectations; she needs the dangerous mountains not marriage in the valley—marriage would leave her restless, it would never last.

(Pause.)

PROPRIETRESS: *(Dryly.)* Well, then…you were both satisfied…

(As he turns to her, surprised.)

…with what you had.

MAN: That's a surprise—I never thought of that. Yes; very nearly. *(Thinks further.)* Almost. Yes. *(Slight pause.)* That's a shock, now.

PROPRIETRESS: To realize that you were almost perfectly happy.

MAN: Almost—You see, there was always—of necessity—something so tentative about it and uncertain, that I never thought of it as perfect, but it was—a perfect chaos. Amazing.

PROPRIETRESS: And your wife?

MAN: *(Slight pause.)* My wife is who I should be married to. We've always helped one another. I'll always be grateful for having her. Especially her kindness.

PROPRIETRESS: She's not ambitious.

MAN: Yes; within bounds. We're partners in a business—advisory service for town planners. She's tremendously competent; I oversee; do less and less, though.

PROPRIETRESS: Why? Isn't it important?

MAN: Certainly is—we've changed whole countrysides for the next hundred years.

PROPRIETRESS: Then why do less and less?

MAN: I won't be here in a hundred years—That struck me powerfully one morning.

(Pause.)

PROPRIETRESS: So—all in all—you will survive this.

MAN: *(Catching the implied rebuke.)* That's right. And in a while, whole days will go by when her anguish barely crosses my mind; and then weeks, and then months, I imagine. *(Slight pause.)* And as I say this, I know that at this very moment she may well be keeping herself hidden from me so as not to wound me with her dying.

PROPRIETRESS: Or wound herself.

(He looks at her questioningly.)

PROPRIETRESS: If she doesn't have to look at what she's lost she loses less.— But I don't believe it's as bad as you make it. She's only keeping you away so that you won't see her so frightened of the knife. She has sense.

MAN: But why!—I would try to comfort her!

PROPRIETRESS: *(Strongly, angrily protesting.)* But she doesn't want comfort, she

wants her power back! You came to her for happiness, not some torn flesh bleeding on the sheets! She knows how long pity lasts!
(Slight pause.)

MAN: Then what are you saying?—That there is really no gift I can give her at all?—Is that what you say?
(Proprietress, silent, lowers her eyes.)

There is really nothing between us, is there—nothing but an…uncommitment? *(Grins.)* Maybe that's why it's so hard to think of something to give her…She asked me once—as we were getting up at the end of an evening—she said, "Can you remember all the women you've had?" Because she couldn't remember all her men, she said.

PROPRIETRESS: And did you believe her?

MAN: No. I thought she was merely reassuring me of her indifference—that she'd never become demanding. It chilled me up the spine.

PROPRIETRESS: Really! Why?

MAN: Why say such a thing unless she had a terrific urge to hold onto me?

PROPRIETRESS: But now you've changed your mind…
(He turns to her surprised.)

MAN: No, I kind of think now she was telling the truth. I think there is some flow of indifference in her, cold and remote, like water flowing in a cave. As there is in me. *(Slight pause.)* I feel you're condemning me now.

PROPRIETRESS: I never condemn anyone; you know that. I can't.

MAN: I know. But still, deep, deep down ….

PROPRIETRESS: No. I'm helpless not to forgive everything, finally.

MAN: That's your glory, but in some deepest part of you there has to be some touch of contempt…

PROPRIETRESS: What are you saying?—You carefully offered only your friendship, didn't you?

MAN: But what more could I offer!

PROPRIETRESS: Then you can't expect what you would have had if you'd committed yourself, can you.

MAN: What I would have had…?

PROPRIETRESS: Yes!—To be clung to now, to be worn out with weeping, to be staggered with your new loneliness, to be clarified with grief, washed with it, cleansed by a whole sorrow. A lover has to earn that satisfaction. If you couldn't bring yourself to share her life, you can't expect to share her dying. Is that what you'd like?

MAN: I would like to understand what I was to her.

PROPRIETRESS: *(Protesting.)* You were her friend!

MAN: *(Shakes his head.)* There is no such thing. No! No! No! What is a friend who only wants the good news and the bright side? I love her. But I am forbidden to by my commitments, by my age, by my aching joints—great God almighty, I'm sleepy by half-past nine! The whole thing is ludicrous, what could she have seen in me? I can't bear the sight of my face in the mirror—I'm shaving my father every morning!

PROPRIETRESS: Then why not believe her—you were...simply one of her friends.

MAN: *(Pause.)* One of her...friends. Yes.—I'll have to try to accept that. *(Slight pause.)* But why doesn't it empty me? Why am I still filled like this? What should I do that I haven't done—or say that I haven't said to make some breakthrough? *(Weeping.)* My God, what am I saying! *(Imploring.)* You know. Tell me!

PROPRIETRESS: Perhaps...that it's perfect, just as it is?

(He slowly turns from her, absorbing her voice.)

That it is all that it could ever have become?

(Pause.)

MAN: You feel that?—You believe that?

PROPRIETRESS: Yes.

MAN: ...That we are as close now as we can ever come?

PROPRIETRESS: Yes.—But she believes she's going to make it, she knows she'll live.

MAN: So she's simply...momentarily afraid.

PROPRIETRESS: Oh, terribly, yes.

MAN: *(With gathering hope.)* That's possible; and it's true that she'd never wish to be seen that scared, especially by me. She has contempt for cowardice, she rises to any show of bravery—any! I think you're possibly right; she'll want to see me when she's made it! When she's a winner again!

PROPRIETRESS: I'm sure of it.

MAN: On the other hand... *(Breaks off suddenly; as though a hollowness opens beneath him his face goes expressionless.)* ...it's also possible, isn't it... that...

PROPRIETRESS: *(Cutting him off, with dread.)* Why go further? You'll know everything soon.

MAN: Not if I can't see her. She won't say the name of the hospital.

PROPRIETRESS: *(She touches his hand.)* But why go further?

MAN: But if she...dies?

PROPRIETRESS: She doesn't expect to.

MAN: *(With confidence, an awareness.)* Or she does expect to.

(And he turns to her; she is filled with love and anguish; he speaks directly to her, gripping her hand in his.)

Either way, my being with her now...would only deepen it between us when it should not be deepened, because very soon now I will be far too old. If she makes it…it would not be good for us—to have shared such agony. It won't cure age, nothing will—*That's* it.

(She offers her lips, he kisses her.)

It's that she doesn't want it spoiled you see, by deepening.

PROPRIETRESS: *(She embraces him, her body pressed to his, an immense longing in it and a sense of a last embrace.)* She wants to make it stay exactly as it is…forever. *(She presses his face to hers, they kiss.)* How gently!

(He kisses her again. With a near cry of farewell.)

Oh how gently!

(He slips from her embrace; a new thought as he looks around the shop.)

MAN: Then what I ought to send her is something she could definitely keep for a long time. *(He is quickened as he looks about, as though he almost knows beforehand what to seek. He moves more quickly from object to object, and at a tray of costume jewelry he halts, draws out a watch on a gold chain.)* Does this work? *(Winds it.)*

PROPRIETRESS: Oh yes, it's exact. It's an antique.

MAN: *(Puts the watch to his ear, then couches it in his hand, hefts it, then hangs it from the neck of the Proprietress and stands back to look at it on her.)* Yes, it's beautiful.

PROPRIETRESS: I know.

(He starts to take out his wallet.)

Take it.

(She takes it off her neck and holds it out, hanging it before him; he puts back his wallet. The implication freezes him.)

Go ahead—it's just the right thing; it will tell her to be brave each time she looks at it.

(He takes the watch and chain and looks at them in his hand.)

You never said her name. *(She starts to smile.)*

MAN: *(Starting to smile.)* You never said yours. *(Slight pause.)* Thank you. Thank you…very much.

(On each of their faces a grin spreads—of deep familiarity. The light begins to lower; with the smile still on his face he moves away from the setting until he is facing front, staring. The woman and the boutique go dark, vanishing. He strolls away, alone.)

THE END

The Adoption

BY JOYCE CAROL OATES

THE AUTHOR

Joyce Carol Oates is the author of a number of plays including the recent *Cry Me a River,* produced in Cambridge, Massachusetts and *The Eclipse,* produced in Stockholm, Sweden. Originally produced at the American Place Theatre, *I Stand Before You Naked* has been performed numerous times in the United States and abroad. Plays of hers have also been performed at the Humana Festival in Louisville, the McCarter Theatre in Princeton, and Ensemble Studio Theatre in New York. Her novel *Black Water,* from which the opera was adapted, was published in 1992 and was a finalist for both the Pulitzer Prize and the National Book Critics Circle Award.

She has received awards from the Guggenheim Foundation, the National Institute of Arts and Letters, the Lotus Club, and is a member of the American Academy and Institute of Arts and Letters. For many years her short stories have been included in the annual Best American Short Stories and the O'Henry Prize stories collections, and she has twice been the recipient of the O'Henry Special Award for Continuing Achievement. She is the 1996 recipient of the PEN/Malamud Award for a lifetime of achievement in the short story form, joining such previous winners as William Maxwell, Grace Paley, and Peter Taylor.

Born in Lockport, New York, she was educated at Syracuse University and the University of Wisconsin. Joyce Carol Oates is married and lives in Princeton, New Jersey, where she is the Roger S. Berlind Distinguished Professor in the Humanities at Princeton University.

ORIGINAL PRODUCTION

The Adoption was originally produced at The Ensemble Studio Theatre, May 1996. It was directed by Kevin Confoy, John Handy as Stage Manager, with the following cast:

MRS. . . . . Cecilia DeWolf
MR. . . . . Dan Dailey
X. . . . . Donna Mervin
NABBO. . . . . Margo Skinner
NADBO . . . . Tara Sands

CHARACTERS
MR.: a Caucasian man in his late 30s or early 40s
MRS.: a Caucasian woman of about the same age
X: male or female, of any mature age
NABBO: a child
NADBO: a "twin" of Nabbo

PLACE
An adoption agency office. Sterile surroundings, merely functional furnishings. Prominent on the wall facing the audience is a large clock with a minute hand of the kind that visibly "jumps" from minute to minute. At the start, the clock measures real time; by subtle degrees, it begins to accelerate.

TIME
The present.

Lights up. We have been hearing bright, cheery music ("It's a Lovely Day Today") which now subsides. Mr. and Mrs. are seated side by side, gripping hands; they appear excited and apprehensive. They are conventionally well-dressed, as if for church, and do indeed exude a churchy aura. Mr. has brought a briefcase, Mrs. a "good" purse. A large bag (containing children's toys) close by. To the left of Mr. and Mrs. is a door in the wall; to the right, behind them, is the clock. With lights up the clock begins its ticking, the time at 11:00.

MRS.: I'm so excited—*frightened!*

MR.: It's the day we've been waiting for—I'm sure.

MRS.: Oh, do you *think*—? I don't dare to hope.

MR.: They *were* encouraging, last time—

MRS.: Yes, they were!

MR.: They wouldn't send us away empty-handed again—would they?

MRS.: Well, they did last time, and the time before last—

MR.: But this *is* going to be different, I'm sure. They *hinted*—

MRS.: No, they all but *said—promised—*

MR.: —um, not a *promise* exactly, but—

MRS.: It was, it was a promise!—almost. In all but words.

MR.: Yes. They *hinted*—today is the day.

MRS.: *(On her feet, too excited to remain seated.)* The day we've been await-ing—for so long!

MR.: *(On his feet.) So* long!

MRS.: I feel like a, a bride again! A—virgin! *(Giggles.)*

MR.: *(Touching or embracing her.)* You *look* like a *madonna.*

MRS.: It's a, a—delivery—

MR.: *(Subtle correction.)* A *deliverance.*

MRS.: *(Euphoric, intense.)* We can't just live for ourselves alone. A woman, a man—

MR.: *(Emphatically.)* That's selfish.

MRS.: That's—unnatural.

MR.: Lonely.

MRS.: *(Wistfully.) So* lonely.

MR.: A home without—

MRS.: —children—

MR.: —is *empty.*

MRS: Not what you'd call a "home"—

MR.: But we have means, we can afford to "extend our boundaries."

MRS.: Thank God! *(Eyes uplifted, sincerely.)*

MR.: *(Glance upward.)* Yes, indeed—thank You, God. *(Pause.)* Of course, um—we're not millionaires. Just, um—"comfortable."

MRS.: —"comfortable Americans"—

MR.: —of the "educated" class—"middle class"—

MRS.: Oh, dear—aren't we "upper-middle"? Your salary—

MR.: *(Finger to lips, stern.)* We are *not* millionaires.

MRS.: Well—we've "paid off our mortgage," we have a "tidy little nest egg," we've made "sensible, long-term investments"—

MR.: *(Cautioning.)* We are what you'd call *medium comfortable.* We can afford to extend our boundaries, and begin a—family.

MRS.: *(Almost tearful.)* A family! After twelve years of waiting!

MR.: *(Counting rapidly on fingers.)* Um—thirteen, darling.

MRS.: *(Belatedly realizing what she has said.)* I mean—twelve years of *marriage.* Not just *waiting. (Glances at Mr.)* Oh—thirteen?

MR.: *(Defensive.)* -We've been happy, of course. Our marriage hasn't been merely *waiting*—

MRS.: —for a, a baby—

MR.: —a family—

MRS.: *(Cradling gesture with her arms.)* —a darling little *baby*—

MR.: —strapping young *son*—

MRS.: *(Emphatically.)* We've done plenty of other things!

MR.: Certainly have! Hobbies, travel— *(A bit blank.)* —paying off our mortgage—

MRS.: *(Grimly.)* We've been happy. We love each other, after all.

MR.: Sure do! Sweetest gal in the world! *(Kisses Mrs.'s cheek.)*

MRS.: *(Repeating in same tone.)* We've been happy.

MR.: Damned happy.

MRS.: We have snapshots to prove it—

MR.: Albums of snapshots to prove it!

(A pause. Mr. and Mrs. glance nervously at the clock.)

MRS.: *(A soft voice.)* Of course, every now and then—

MR.: —in the interstices of happiness—

MRS.: —between one heartbeat and the next—

MR.: -in the early, insomniac hours of the morning, maybe—

MRS.: —in the bright-lit maze of the food store—

MR.: —like fissures of deep, sharp shadow at noon—

MRS.: —we have sometimes, for maybe just a—

MR.: —fleeting second—

MRS.: —teensy-weensy fleeting *second*—

MR.: —been a bit lonely.

    (Pause.)

MRS.: *(Sad, clear voice.)* So lonely.

    (Pause. The door opens, and X appears. X is a bureaucrat, in conventional office attire; may wear rimless glasses; carries a clipboard containing numerous documents. He/She is impersonally "friendly.")

X: *(Bright smile, loud voice.)* Goooood morning! *(Consults clipboard.)* You are—Mr. and Mrs.—?

MR. AND MRS.: *(Excited, hopeful.)* That's right! *(Mrs. quickly straightens Mr.'s necktie, which has become crooked.)*

X: *(Making a production of shaking hands.)* Mr.—! Mrs.—! Soooo glad to meet you.

MRS.: *(Flushed, hand to bosom.)* So g-glad to meet *you.*

MR.: Is this the— *(Fearful of asking "is this the day".)* —the right time?

X: No time like the present! That's agency policy.

MRS.: An—excellent policy.

MR.: *(Nodding.)* Very excellent.

X: And you're punctual, Mr. and Mrs.—, I see. A good sign.

MR.: Oh, we're very punctual.

MRS.: *(Breathless.)* Always have been!

MR.: We've been here since 7:45 A.M., actually. When the custodial staff unlocked the building.

MRS.: We came to the c-city last night. We're staying in a hotel.

MR.: —a medium-priced hotel!—

MRS.: We were terrified of missing our appointment—

MR.: *(Chiding Mrs.)* We were not *terrified,* we were—vigilant.

MRS.: Yes, vigilant—

X: It *is* wise to be punctual. Such details in perspective parents are meticulously noted. *(Mysteriously taps documents.)*

MR.: *(A deep breath.)* And…is…today…the…d-day?

MRS.: *(A hand on Mr.'s arm, faintly echoing.)* —the d-day?

X: *(Beaming.)* Yes. Today *is* your day, Mr. and Mrs.—. Your application to adopt one of our orphans has been fully processed by our board of directors, and approved. Congratulations!

MRS.: Oh—! Oh!

MR.: Oh my God!

    (Mr. and Mrs. clasp hands, thrilled. X strides to the door, opens it with a flourish, and leads in Nabbo.)

X: Here he is, Mr. and Mrs.—your baby.

MR. AND MRS.: *(Faintly.)* "Our baby!"

(Nabbo is perhaps eight years old. He wears a mask to suggest deformity or disfigurement, but the mask should be extremely lifelike and not exaggerated. His skin is an ambiguous tone—dusky or mottled, not "black." He may be partly bald as well, as if his scalp has been burnt. He has a mild twitch or tremor. Mr. and Mrs. stare at Nabbo, who stares impassively at them.)

X: *(Rubbing hands together.)* So! Here we are! Here we have "Nabbo." *(Nudging him.)* Say hello to your new mother and father, Nabbo. *(Nabbo is silent.)*

MR. AND MRS.: H-Hello!

X: *(A bit coercive.)* Say "hello" to your new mother and father, Nabbo. "Hel-lo."

(Nabbo is silent.)

MR.: *(Hesitantly.)* He isn't a, an actual—*baby*—is he?

X: *(Consulting document.)* Nabbo is eight months old. To the day.

MR.: Eight *months*—?

MRS.: Oh but he's—so sweet. So—

X: Our records are impeccable.

MRS.: —*childlike.* So—

MR.: *(A bit doubtful, to X.)* What did you say his name is?

MRS.: —*trusting.* So—

X: "Nabbo." "NAB-BO." *(Equal stress on both syllables.)*

MRS.: —needful of our love!

(X pushes Nabbo toward Mr. and Mrs. He is weakly resistant.)

MR. AND MRS.: "Nab-bo"—?

X: *(Brightly urging Nabbo.)* "Hel-lo!"

(Nabbo remains silent. Visible tremor.)

MR.: Maybe he doesn't know—English?

MRS.: Of course he doesn't, that's the problem. *(Speaking loudly, brightly.)* Hel-lo, Nab-bo! You've come a long distance to us, haven't you? Don't be frightened. We are your new Mommy and your Daddy— *(Points to herself and to Mr.)* We'll teach you everything you need to know.

MR.: We sure will!

(Mr. has taken a camera out of his briefcase and takes pictures of Mrs. posing with Nabbo. Nabbo is rigid with terror of the flash.)

MR.: Beau-ti-ful! The first *minute* of our new life. *(Takes another picture.)*

MRS.: This is a holy time. I feel God's presence here.

MR.: *(To X, hesitantly.)* Excuse me, but is Nabbo a, um—little boy, or a little girl?

MRS.: *(Gently poking Mr.)* Dear, don't be crude!

MR.: I'm only curious.

X: *(Checking document, frowning.)* You didn't specify, did you? You checked "either sex."

MRS.: *(Eagerly.)* Oh yes, oh yes! "Either."

MR.: *(Protesting.)* Hey, I was just curious. I'm Daddy, after all.

MRS.: *(Fussing over Nabbo, squatting beside him.)* He's "Daddy," dear; and I'm "Mommy." We've waited so long for you! Only for *you*, dear. Can you say "Daddy"—"Mommy"?

(Nabbo remains silent, twitching slightly.)

MR.: *(As if Nabbo is deaf.)* "DAD-DY"—"MOM-MY"—

MRS.: *(Her ear to Nabbo's mouth, but hears nothing.)* Of course, you're shy; you've come such a long distance.

MR.: *(Solemnly.)* From the "dark side of the Earth."

MRS.: *(To Mr., chiding.)* Don't be so—grim, dear. That isn't the right tone. *(To Nabbo; singing.)* "Little Baby Bunting! Daddy's gone a-hunting! Gone to get a new fur skin! To wrap the Baby Bunting in!"

MR.: *(Joining in.)* "—wrap the Baby Bunting in!" *(Laughs, rubs hands happily together.)* I can't believe this is *real*.

MRS.: *(To Nabbo.)* Now, Naddo—

MR.: "Nab-bo"—

MRS.: That's what I said: "Nad-do."

MR.: Dear, it's "Nab-bo."

MRS.: "Nab-bo"? That's what I *said*. My goodness! *(She turns to the bag, removing a large doll from it.)* Look, Nabbo darling—just for *you*. Isn't she lovely?

(Urging Nabbo to take the doll, but Nabbo is motionless, not lifting his/her arms.)

MR.: *(Taking a shiny toy firetruck out of the bag; in a hearty "masculine" voice.)* Nabbo, look what Daddy has for you. Cool, eh? *(Running the truck vigorously along the floor, making "engine" noises deep in his throat.)* RRRRRRRMMMMMMMM! Cool, Nabbo, eh?

X: *(Holding out the clipboard and a pen.)* Excuse me, "Mommy" and "Daddy": please sign on the dotted line, and Nabbo is yours forever.

MRS.: Oh, yes!

MR.: Of course!

(As Mr. takes the pen to sign, however, X suddenly draws back. As if he/she has just remembered.)

X: Um—one further detail.

MR. AND MRS.: Yes? What?

X: It appears that—Nabbo has a twin.

MR. AND MRS.: *(Blankly.)* A—twin?

X: From whom Nabbo is said to be inseparable.

MR. AND MRS.: "Inseparable"—?

X: They must be adopted together, you see.

MR. AND MRS.: *(Trying to comprehend.)* Twin—?
  (The minute hand of the clock continues to accelerate.)

X: Yes. An identical twin.

MR.: *Identical?* Like our *c-child?*

X: Frequently, our adoptees are from large lit— *(About to say "litter," changes his/her mind.)* —families. *(Pause.)* The term "twin" is merely generic.

MRS.: I don't understand. Isn't our Nabbo one of a kind?

X: Nabbo is indeed one of a kind; we are all "one of a kind." But Nabbo also has a twin, from whom Nabbo is inseparable.

MR.: But—what does that mean?

MRS.: "Inseparable—"?
  (Pause. Mr., Mrs. stare at each other.)

MR.: *(Suddenly, extravagant.)* Hell, I'm game! *(Throws arms wide.)*

MRS.: *(Squeals with excitement, kneeling before Nabbo.)* You have a *twin,* Nabbo? Another just like you?

MR.: *(Recklessly.)* Two for the price of one, eh?

MRS.: *(Faint, laughing, peering up at Mr.)* Oh, but—"Daddy"—are we prepared? We've never had *one,* and now—*two?*

MR.: Isn't that the way twins always come—in *twos?* Surprising Mommy and Daddy? *(Laughs.)*

MRS.: *(Dazed, euphoric.)* Oh yes oh yes oh *yes! (Pause, voice drops.)* I'm afraid. *(Pause.)*

MR.: *I'm* afraid. Gosh.

X: I regret to say, Mr. and Mrs.—, that our agency requires, in such a situation, that adoptive parents take in both siblings. For, given the fact of "identical twins," there can be no justification in adopting one instead of the other.

MRS.: That's…so.

MR.: *(Wiping face with handkerchief.)* You got us there…yes!
  (X takes Nabbo's arm as if to lead him back through the door.)

X: *(Somber voice.)* There are so many deserving applicants registered with our agency, you see. Our waiting list is years long.

MRS.: *(Desperate.)* Oh—oh, wait—

MR.: Hey, wait—

MRS.: *(Hugging Nabbo.)* We want them both—of course.

MR.: *(Wide, dazed grin.) I'm* game!—Did I say that?

X: *(Severely.)* You're certain, Mr. and Mrs.—?

MR. AND MRS.: Yes! Yes!

X: *(Goes to the door, opens it and leads in Nadbo, with some ceremony.)* This, Mr. and Mrs.—, is "Nad-bo."

MR. AND MRS.: *(A bit numbed.)* "NAD-BOO."

X: "NAD-BO."

MR. AND MRS.: "NAD-*BO.*"

(Nabbo and Nadbo, twins, stand side by side. They exhibit identical twitches and tremors, cowering together.)

MRS.: *(Voice airy, strange.)* What a long long distance you have come to us— Nab-bo, Nad-bo! Yet we were fated.

MR.: From "the dark side of the Earth"—from "the beginning of Time."
(Mr., Mrs. behave like doting parents, fussing over the twins.)

MRS.: We'll teach you the English language—

MR.: *American* English language—greatest language on Earth!

MRS.: We'll bring you to our home—

MR.: *Your* home, now—

MRS.: We'll love love love you so you forget whatever it is— *(Pause, a look of distaste.)* —you've escaped.

MR.: *That's* for sure! No looking back.

MRS.: No looking back, you'll be American children. *No* past!

MR.: We're your new Mommy and Daddy—know what that means?

MRS.: *(Pointing.)* He's "Daddy"—I'm "Mommy"—

MR.: *(Overlapping, hearty.)* I'm "Mommy"—he's "Daddy"—

MRS.: *(Lightly chiding.)* I'm "Mommy."

MR.: *(Quickly.)* I mean—I'm "Daddy." Of course!

MRS.: *(Taking out of the bag a cap with bells.)* I knitted this myself, for you! *(Pause.)* Oh dear—there's only one. *(Mrs. fits the cap awkwardly on Nabbo's head; takes out a sweater.)* Thank goodness, I knitted this, too— *(Nadbo takes the sweater from her, puts it over his head.)*

MR.: You'll have to knit matching sets, dear. From now on everything must be in duplicate.

X: *(Smiling, but with authority.)* Hmmm! I do need your signatures, Mr. and Mrs.—, before the adoption procedure can continue.
(Mr. wheels in a tricycle. Both children snatch at it, push at each other. The child who gets it, however, has no idea what it is, and struggles with it, knocking it over, attacking the wheels. Mr. pulls in a wagon. Similar action.)

MRS.: Oh!—I nearly forgot. You must be starving—having come so far! *(Takes fudge out of bag.)* I made this chocolate-walnut fudge just yesterday!
(Nabbo, Nadbo take pieces of proffered fudge; taste it hesitantly; begin to eat, ravenously; spit mouthfuls out.)

MRS.: Oh, dear! *(With a handkerchief, dabbing at their faces.)* You mustn't be greedy, you know. There's plenty to eat here.
(Nabbo, Nadbo snatch at the rest of the fudge, shoving pieces into their mouths, though they are sickened by it, and soon spit it out again. Nadbo has a minor choking fit.)

MR.: *(With camera.)* O.K., guys! Everybody smile! Say "MON KEE!"
(Mrs. embraces the children, smiling radiantly at the camera. The children cringe at the flash.)

MRS.: This is the happiest day of my life. Thank you, God.

MR.: This is the happiest day of *my* life.
(Mr. hands X the camera so that he/she can take a picture of the new family. Mr., Mrs. smiling broadly, Nabbo and Nadbo cringing. Nadbo tries to hide under the sweater, and Mrs. gently removes it.)

MR.: Thanks!

X: *(Handing camera back to Mr.)* Lovely. Now, we should complete our procedure. Your signatures, please—

MR. AND MRS.: Yes, yes of course....
(Again, X draws the clipboard back out of their reach, at the crucial moment.)

X: Ummm—just a moment. *(Peering at a document.)* I'm afraid— Nabbo and Nadbo have a third sibling.
(Mr. has taken the pen from X's hand, and now drops it.)

MRS.: *(Faint, hand to bosom.)* A *third...?*

MR.: ...another *twin?*

X: *(Hesitant.)* Not "twin" exactly. With these high-fertility races, the precise clinical term is—too clinical. Let's say "identical sibling."

MR.: Tri-tri-triplets?

X: Not "triplets," exactly. *(Evasively.)* "Identical sibling" is preferred.

MRS.: *(Vague, voice strange.)* Oooohhh another of you!—how, how— how *wonderful.* Your mother must be—must have been— *(Draws a blank.)* —if you had one, I mean. Nab-bo, Nab-do—I mean, Nad-do—?

(Nabbo, Nadbo poke each other, but do not speak. Cap bells jingle. One shoves at the shiny firetruck, or the wagon. The other finds a piece of fudge and pops it into his mouth.)

MR.: *(Awkward, dazed, to X.)* B-but I'm afraid—we really *can't,* you know. Not three. We'd only prepared for *one.*

MRS.: When we left home yesterday—to drive here—we'd only prepared— enough diapers, a single bassinet— *(Pause; a kind of wildness comes over her.)* A third? A third *baby?* Is it possible? I *did* always want a large family...

MR.: But, darling, not in five minutes!

MRS.: We can buy a new house. More bedrooms! Bunkbeds! A bigger family room! *(Pause, breathing quickly.)* I was so lonely in my parents' house— just the *one* of me. And everything done *for me.* Never a moment's want or deprivation... *(Pause.)* My mother was from a large family—eight children. Dozens of grandchildren.

MR.: But not in five minutes!

MRS.: *(Turning on him, cutting.)* What difference does that make? We've been infertile—*sterile*—for fourteen years. We've got a lot of catching up to do!

MR.: *(Wincing.)* Thirteen years...

MRS.: *(Laughing, trying to hug Nabbo and Nadbo.)* Here is our— deliverance! These "tragic orphans"—"from the dark side of the Earth." Human beings can't live for themselves alone...

MR.: *(Gripping Mrs. by the shoulders.)* Darling, please! You're hysterical. You're not—yourself.

MRS.: *(Shrilly.)* Who am I, then? Who am I, then?

MR.: Darling!—

(Nabbo and Nadbo have been cringing fearfully.)

X: *(With authority.)* Mr.—, Mrs.—? I'm afraid your allotted time has nearly transpired. Even as you dally— *(X indicates the clock.)* —this past hour, 110,273 new "tragic orphans" have been, as it's said, "born."

MRS.: *(Hand to bosom.)* How many?—my goodness!

MR.: I think we've been cruelly misled here. I strongly object to being manip- ulated!

X: If you had troubled to read the agency's restrictions and guidelines hand- book, Mr.—, more closely, you would not affect such surprise now.

MR.: I did read it! I've practically memorized it! We've been on your damned waiting list for a decade!

MRS.: *(Vague, intense, to X.)* There is a—a third sibling?—identical with our b-babies?

X: Identical DNA, chromosomes—identical faces and bodies. But, you know, not "identical" inwardly. In the soul.

MRS.: "The soul—!" *(A strange expression on her face as of radiance, pain.)*

MR.: *(Awkward, flush-faced.)* Darling, it's just that we—can't. We don't have room—

MRS.: Of course we have room!

MR.: We don't have resources—

MRS.: Of course we have resources!

MR.: *(Tugging at his necktie, panting.)* We're practically in *debt—paupers—*

MRS.: *(Extravagantly, arms wide.)* We're wealthy!—we have infinite space— inwardly.

MR.: Inwardly?

MRS.: The soul is infinite, isn't it? *Mine* is, isn't *yours?*

MR.: *(Baffled.)* My—*soul? Where*—?

MRS.: *(Tugging at X's arm.)* You tell him! The soul is infinite, isn't it? "The Kingdom of God is within"—space that goes on forever!
(Mrs. has been working herself up into an emotional state; Nabbo and Nadbo are frightened of her. They cast off the cap, sweater, etc., shove away the tricycle; begin to make mournful keening sounds and rock back and forth, their small bodies hunched. X scolds them inaudibly; they make a break for the closed door, and X grabs their arms to stop them.)

MRS.: What?—where are you going? Nab-bo—no, you're Nad-bo—I mean Nab-do—Nab-*boo*—come here! be good! you're ours, aren't you? Mommy loves you *so much*— *(Tries to embrace children, who resist her.)*

MR.: *(Blank, dazed smile.)* Daddy loves you so much! *(Pushes the tricycle back.)* Since the beginning of Time!

MRS.: Since *before* the beginning of Time—
(Nabbo and Nadbo cower, hiding behind X, who is annoyed at the turn of events, surreptitiously slapping at the children or gripping their shoulders forcibly. The mourning-keening sounds seem to be coming from all over.)

MRS.: *(Hands to ears.)* Oh, what is that sound! It hurts my ears—

MR.: Nab-boo! Nad-doo! Bad boys! *Stop that!*

X: *(Threatening children.)* It's just some village dirge—nothing! Pay no attention!

MRS.: It's coming from here, too—
(Impulsively rushes to the door and opens it, steps through; X immediately pulls her back.)

X: *(Furious.)* Mrs.—! This door can only be opened by authorized agency personnel! *(X shuts the door.)*

(Mrs. has recoiled back into the room. Hand over her mouth, she staggers forward as if about to collapse.)

MR.: *(Rushing to help her.)* Darling? What is it?

X: That door was *not* to be opened. I could call a security guard and have you arrested, Mrs.—! Taken out of here in handcuffs!

MRS.: *(Eyes shut, nauseated.)* Oh…oh…

MR.: Darling, what did you see?

X: *(Loudly.)* Mrs.— saw *nothing*. There was *nothing* to be seen.

MR.: Darling—?

MRS.: *(Feeble whisper, leaning on Mr.'s arm.)* Take them back. We don't want them.

MR.: What did you see, darling? What's behind that door?

MRS.: *(Trying to control rising hysteria.)* Take them back. We don't want them. Any of them. I want to go *home*.

X: Hmmm! I thought so. Poor risks for adoption.

MR.: Darling, are you certain? We've waited so long…*prayed* so long…

MRS.: *(A small scream.)* Take them away! All of them! *(Hides eyes.)* We're not strong enough—

X: *(Coldly.)* You're certain, Mr. and Mrs——? You can never again apply with our agency, you know.

MRS.: Take them away!

MR.: *(Trying to speak in normal voice.)* We're sorry—so sorry—

(X marches Nabbo and Nadbo out, and the door is shut behind them.)

MR.: *(Weakly, belatedly calling after.)* Um—so sorry—

(The mourning-keening sound grows louder. Mr. and Mrs. freeze; lights dim except on the clock face, where the minute hand continues its accelerated progress. Lights out. Mourning sound ceases. Lights up on Mr. and Mrs., who have come forward. Darkness elsewhere. The clock is no longer visible. Mr. and Mrs. speak in a duet of agitated rhythms, overlappings, a strange music that should suggest, though not too overtly mimic, the mourning-keening sound. This conclusion should be elegiac, a barely restrained hysteria; but it is restrained.)

MRS.: *(Hands to her face.)* What have we done!—

MR.: It was a, a wise decision—

MRS.: —necessary—

MR.: —necessary decision—

MRS.: Waited all our lives— Oh, what have we done—

MR.: It was your decision—

MRS.: Our day of birth—delivery—

MR.: *Deliverance*—

MRS.: —weren't strong enough—

MR.: *You* weren't— *I* was— *(Pause.)* —*wasn't*—

MRS.: What have we done!—not strong enough—

MR.: Who the hell *is* strong enough I'd like to know—

MRS.: God didn't make us strong enough—

MR.: —rational decision, necessary—

MRS.: —necessary— *(Clutching at her womb.)* Oh! Oh what have we done! My babies—

MR.: *(Anguished, strikes chest with fist.)* I'm only human! What can I do! Who can forgive me? *(Pause, peers into audience.)* Who *isn't* human? You cast the first stone!

MRS.: *(Hands framing face.)* That corridor!—that space!—to the horizon!—so many! And the *smell. (Nauseated.)*

MR.: *(Reasoning.)* There isn't room in the heart—I mean the *home*—the *house!*—no matter how many bunkbeds. We're not paupers!—I mean, we're not millionaires. Who's been saying we *are?*

MRS.: *(Confused.)* Bunkbeds?—how many?

MR.: How many? *(Rapidly counting on fingers, confused.)*

MRS.: *(A soft cry.)* Our home—*house!*—empty!—

MR.: *(Protesting.)* Hey: there's *us.*

MRS.: So lonely!—

MR.: Rational, necessary decision—no choice.

MRS.: *So* lonely—

MR.: Look, I refuse to be manipulated, to be made *guilty*—

MRS.: So many years waiting, and so lonely—

MR.: *(Pleading.)* Who the hell *isn't* human? I ask you!

MRS.: *(Has found the knitted cap on the floor, picks it up lovingly, bells chime.)* God knows, God sees into the heart. Forgive us, God—

MR.: We had no choice.

MRS.: —no choice!

MR.: And we're *not* millionaires!
      (Lights begin to fade.)

MRS.: *(Waving, tearful and smiling.)* Goodbye Nabbo!—Nadbo!— Nabdo?— dear, innocent babies! Mommy loved you so!

MR.: *(Waving, ghastly smile.)* Goodbye, boys! Sons! Your Daddy loved you so!

MRS.: Don't think ill of us, don't forget us! Goodbye!

MR.: Goodbye, sons! Be brave!

MRS.: *(Blowing kisses.)* Mommy loved you so! Goodbye!

MR. AND MRS.: Goodbye, goodbye, goodbye!

    (Lights out.)

THE END

Bel Canto

BY WILL SCHEFFER

I lived for beauty…I lived for love…why is this happening to me?
Puccini's "Vissi d'arte" from TOSCA

Together Wendy we can live with the sadness
I'll love you with all the madness in my soul
Someday girl I don't know when
We're gonna get to that place
Where we really want to go
And we'll walk in the sun
But till then tramps like us
Baby we were born to run
Springsteen's "Putani come noi" from BORN TO RUN

Chaste goddess, as you cast a silver light
On these ancient and sacred trees
Turn your lovely face to us
Unclouded and unveiled
Ah, YES!

Bellini's "Casta diva" from NORMA

THE AUTHOR
Plays: *Easter* (Naked Angels), *Tennessee and Me* (EST Marathon '97, Tennessee Williams Festival '98), *Bel Canto* (EST Marathon '96), *Falling Man* (EST marathon '94 – selected for the Penguin/Viking book of Gay Plays), *Multiple Personality* (New Works Now: Joseph Papp Public Theater), *Latenight with Commercial Break* (Red Earth Ensemble: Westbeth Theater Center). Television/Film: *In the Gloaming* staring Glen Close and directed by Christopher Reeve for HBO/NYC nominated for five Emmys including Best Television Movie, nominated for WGA Writing Award, winner of CableAce Award for Ourstanding Achievement in Writing. Also for HBO/NYC: *Home* (co-producer). *Paradise* for HBO Pictures. *Ellis Island* (creator of the one-hour dramatic series) for Tom Fontana/Barry Levinson Productions and CBS. Will has taught theater for Lewis and Clark College and playwriting at the Ensemble Studio Theatre. His plays have been produced and/or work-shopped across the country and at such theaters as: Playwright's Horizons, Naked Angels, The Actors Studio (member), Ensemble Studio Theater (member) and The Public Theater. He was selected to be one of the members of the Joseph Papp Public Theater's First Emerging Playwright's Lab in 1994 and the same year was chosen by the HBO New Writer's Project as one of ten new writers of exceptional promise. *Easter* is a recipient of a Pilgrim Project Award and is currently being produced as a feature film.

ORIGINAL PRODUCTION
Bel Canto was first produced at The Ensemble Studio Theatre, May 1996. It was directed by Brian Mertes with the following cast:

Maria Romani (Ma) . . . . Phyllis Sommerville
Philamena Romani (Phil) . . . . Elisabeth Berridge
Virginia Romani (Vinnie) . . . . Fiona Gallagher

CHARACTERS
MARIA ROMANI (MA): 52. But looks older. She is confined to a wheelchair. She has had a partial laryngectomy.

PHILAMENA ROMANI (PHIL): 29. Ma's older daughter. She is a very *big* girl. Her eyes were made for keeping secrets.

VIRGINIA ROMANI (VINNIE): 25. Ma's younger daughter. It is only her surface that looks, talks and acts like the perfect caricature of a "Jersey Girl." She can hold her liquor.

PLACE

The cellar of a small house in Long Beach, New Jersey.

TIME

September 16, 1987. The night of Hurricane Maria. Midnight till morning.

"VISSI D'ARTE"

We hear a storm approaching. Maria Callas sings "Vissi d'arte." A bare light bulb fades up. The light bulb swings gently on a string from the ceiling. It illuminates a small cellar filled mostly with objects that have outlived their usefulness. It's as if the room has faded, has lost all of its color. A rusted, little girl's bike lays on its side. Rickety shelves are lined with fishing poles, tackle boxes, old paint cans, canvas tarps and cobwebs. Empty and half empty boxes are scattered around. In contrast to this sea of detritus and obsolescence, someone has recently carved out a niche of cleanliness and order. A folding table has been set up under the swaying light bulb. A broom and two folding chairs lean against it. On the table there are candles, a flashlight, bedding, a pile of blankets and a boom box/radio. Next to the table there are some cardboard boxes stacked in an organized fashion. Also: a large jug of water, plastic cups, napkins, two six-packs of Diet Coke and a clearly labeled case of 'King Olaf' smoked oysters. The howling wind sneaks through the sash of small opaque storm window. A narrow wooden stairway leads up to the door to the kitchen/bathroom. A wheelchair sits at the bottom of the staircase. The door opens, light slashes down the stairs. Maria hits a high note. Thunder.

PHIL: *(From off-stage.)* Alright Ma, so you sure you don't have to go to the bathroom—

MA: *(From off.)* No.

PHIL: *(Off.)* You're sure—?

MA: *(Off.)* N.O. NO.

PHIL: *(Off.)* Alright. So here we go—

MA: *(Off.)* So alright already.

PHIL: *(Off.)* So alright…

(The sound of Phil struggling to lift Ma. Then: Ma's legs come through the door; Enter Phil navigating Ma down the stairs; slowly.)

MA: Now careful.

PHIL: I know—

MA: VERY careful.

PHIL: Alright.

MA: *(Halfway down.)* Wait!

PHIL: *(Stops.)* What's wrong?

MA: I changed my mind.

PHIL: What—

MA: I have to go.

PHIL: Oh Ma—

MA: So big deal.

PHIL: *(A breath.)* Okay so—

MA: So alright.

(Phil navigates Ma back up the stairs.)

MA: *(Points to the boom box.)* Careful careful—and turn that crap off.

PHIL: I thought—

MA: You thought wrong.

(Phil exits with Ma. From off-stage we hear the following.)

MA: Alright. DOWN.

PHIL: Alright—

MA: Down down down.

PHIL: Alright!

(The sound of water sloshing.)

MA: Jesus, Mary and—

PHIL: I'm sorry—

MA: You are *so* clumsy—

PHIL: I'm sorry already—

MA: Alright. So, GO.

PHIL: Alright.

MA: But leave the door open! *(A beat.)* I SAID TURN THAT CRAP OFF!

(Phil enters. She rushes down the stairs and turns off the boom box. She lets out a deep breath. She unfolds a chair, sits. A moment. She turns on the radio.)

FEMALE ANNOUNCER: "Hurricane Maria is proving to be the worst storm to hit the Eastern seaboard since 1963. Evacuation is a possibility for parts of the New Jersey Shore, stay tuned to this station for further developments—"

MA: *(Off.)* IS THAT HER?! IS SHE BACK?!

PHIL: NO! IT'S THE RADIO!

MA: *(Off.)* SHUT IT OFF!

PHIL: ALRIGHT!

(Phil turns off the radio. She holds her head in her hands. A flush is heard.)

MA: *(Off.)* DONE!

(Phil gets up and walks up the stairs.)

MA: *(Off.)* DONE DONE DONE!

PHIL: I'm coming—

MA: *(Off.)* DONE!

(Phil exits.)

PHIL: *(Off.)* Alright already—

MA: *(Off.)* Alright. So, UP.
> *(The sound of Phil struggling to lift Ma. Ma's legs enter first and then Phil, again slowly navigating the narrow staircase.)*

MA: Now *careful.*

PHIL: I'm trying—
> *(Phil bumps Ma's head into the rafter.)*

MA: OW!

PHIL: I'm sorry—

MA: OW-OW-OW!

PHIL: I'm sorry—

MA: You're trying to kill me!

PHIL: I'm sorry already—

MA: *(A beat.)* So alright.
> *(They start down the staircase again. The phone rings from the kitchen.)*

MA: *(Halfway down.)* Answer the phone!

PHIL: MA!

MA: Down down down and answer the phone!

PHIL: But—

MA: HURRY! CAREFUL! HURRY! OW!
> *(Phil stumbles down the stairs and plops Ma into the wheelchair, then rushes up, exits and answers the phone.)*

PHIL: *(Off.)* Hello?

MA: *(Calls up the stairs.)* IS IT *HER?*
> *(Phil enters holding her hand over the receiver of the phone, she comes down two steps.)*

PHIL: No, it's Aunt Millie—
> *(Ma spins wildly around the cellar in her wheelchair, shakes her head "NO" and looks for a place to hide.)*

PHIL: *(Into the phone.)* No Aunt Millie, she can't talk now—I know. I know. I told her. I'll tell her again. Yeah. We heard. We taped up the windows. Yeah. We're making preparations as we speak. Okay. You too. Bye-bye Aunt Millie.
> *(Phil exits to hang up the phone. She re-enters down the stairs.)*

PHIL: Why do you make me answer the phone when you won't talk to anybody on it?

MA: I thought it was *her.*

PHIL: Aunt Millie wants—

MA: I don't care.

PHIL: She says you're still a young woman—

MA: Meaning what?

PHIL: Meaning you gotta talk to your own sister sooner or later—

MA: No I don't I don't I don't…

PHIL: Oh come on Ma you sound okay—

MA: You shut up!

PHIL: Fine.

> (*The wind is coming up. Phil takes a blanket, stands on a milk crate and stops up the draft. She stills the swaying light.*)

MA: What time is it?

PHIL: It's after Midnight.

MA: Why isn't she back yet?

PHIL: I don't know.

MA: Where did she say she was going?

PHIL: She didn't say.

MA: You didn't ask her!

PHIL: She didn't say.

MA: I want my oysters.

> (*Phil opens the case of 'King Olaf' oysters and gives a tin to Ma. Ma opens the tin and eats the oysters avidly with her fingers.*)

MA: What *did* she say?

PHIL: I already told you.

MA: Tell me again.

PHIL: She said she was going out.

MA: DURING A HURRICANE!!?

PHIL: *(Puts her hands over her ears.)* Please Ma!

MA: What?

PHIL: *(A beat.)* Just don't take it out on—

MA: You didn't try to stop her?

PHIL: It's not like she listens to *me*.

> (*Ma shoves aside the empty tin of oysters. She licks her fingers.*)

MA: You're her big sister! *(Under her breath.)* And getting bigger—

PHIL: So—?

MA: So she should listen to you. You were *supposed* to set an example for her!

PHIL: Ma we don't even *talk* anymore—

MA: *(Aggressively.)* And why is that?

PHIL: I don't know…

MA: Exactly! *(A pause.)* Another.

> (*Phil gives her another tin. Ma opens it; eats. A beat.*)

MA: Tell me again what happened.

PHIL: Oh Jeeze Ma, I already—

MA: TELL ME!

PHIL: Alright. I went to see what was taking her so long in the bathroom like you asked me.

MA: I already know that part.

PHIL: *(A breath.)* And I stood in the hallway and I heard her throwing up her food again—

MA: Now why do you keep saying that?

PHIL: Because it's true.

MA: How do you know that?

PHIL: I hear it.

MA: Maybe you're not hearing it right.

PHIL: I smell it.

MA: What?

PHIL: Half-digested tomato sauce—it's disgusting.

MA: But *why* would she do that?

PHIL: Jesus Ma, to stay *skinny!*

MA: You gotta be kidding me—

PHIL: It's Bulimia!

MA: What is this Bulimia?

PHIL: It's a *sickness.*

MA: It's like "agita"?

PHIL: No. It's *compulsive!*

MA: What is this compulsive?

PHIL: It's—

MA: Another. *(Ma pushes away her empty tin of oysters and points to the case.)*

PHIL: Never mind.

   (Phil gives Ma a tin; Ma eats. A beat. Then emphatically:)

PHIL: She throws up her food to stay thin.

MA: I think you're just jealous.

PHIL: I'm not jealous—

MA: In two years you got fat like the Good Year Blimp—

PHIL: Ma—

MA: Well it's true!

PHIL: Look do you want me to tell you what happened or—

MA: Alright. So, go on!

PHIL: Alright. *(A beat.)* So…she comes out of the bathroom. She's all put together. I can *smell* the hair-spray, the make-up, the nail-polish…the *tomato sauce*—

MA: Alright already—!

PHIL: *(For like the hundredth time.)* I ask her what she's doing. She says: it's none of my business. I say: we're having a hurricane. She says: so what? I say: it's dangerous. She says: I don't care. I say: Ma wants you to come back and finish your dinner. She says: "Oh Brother." She grabs her jacket and starts to walk out the door. I say: where are you going? She says: out. I say: Ma's gonna have a fit. Then she smiles and says: good. *(A beat.)* And then she walks out the door.

(A long pause.)

MA: Good.

PHIL: What good?

MA: You say: *I'll* have a fit and she says: *good?*

PHIL: Come on Ma—

MA: How can she say that?

PHIL: You know how she talks.

MA: How come you told me that part?

PHIL: What.

MA: You *want* to hurt me?

PHIL: She didn't mean it—

MA: Then how come you told me?

PHIL: You ask me to tell you again and again what she—

MA: A *good* daughter wouldn't tell me that part.

PHIL: Ma, please—

MA: Or maybe you're lying.

PHIL: Why would I lie—

MA: Because you hate me.

PHIL: I don't hate you—

MA: You're a liar.

PHIL: I am not a—

MA: You hate me because of what happened with Joey Sclafano!

PHIL: Ma don't start—

MA: You're the one who got *yourself* in trouble. It wasn't *me*—

PHIL: Ma, you promised—

MA: He was a bum, a drifter—if I had let you have that baby…! I saved your *life* is what I did—

PHIL: You know, Jesus Ma, sometimes I swear I could just—

MA: WHAT?

PHIL: Never mind. Just—enough!

MA: *(Accusing, suspicious.)* You never told her nothing, did you?

PHIL: No I never *told*—

MA: Good. *(A beat.)* So now you think that you can turn me *against* her.

PHIL: Why?

MA: Because she's a *doer!* And you sit around here doing nothing all day, listening to that crap, a dreamer, an eater—that's all.

PHIL: Alright. Enough already—

MA: She pays the mortgage!

PHIL: I know—

MA: So where would we be without her, huh? You tell me *that!* Where would we be without *her?*

PHIL: Alright Ma! She's good. She's a good girl. *She's* a good daughter. Alright?

MA: No it's not alright! She *curses* me, she *drinks,* she runs out to do who knows what on a night like tonight—

PHIL: Alright, then she's *bad* Ma!

MA: NO! *You* are the bad one. Just don't forget *that. You* are the bad one.
(Phil is silent. She folds her hands, looks at her lap. Ma continues to glare at her. Phil does not meet her gaze. A moment. Then: Ma pushes aside her empty oyster tin.)

MA: Another.

PHIL: *(Quietly.)* Maybe you should pace yourself.

MA: I'm *hungry.*

PHIL: It's gonna be a long night—

MA: ANOTHER!
(Phil gives another tin to Ma. Ma eats. Phil collects tins and puts them in a plastic bag, hangs it onto Ma's wheelchair. She goes to the boom box.)

MA: Don't even think about it.

PHIL: I just thought it might give your voice a rest—

MA: You worry about yourself. I don't have any regrets. I don't miss cigarettes. I don't miss dancing. I don't miss your father. I don't miss *anything.*
(A pause. Phil sits. Ma eats. Thunder.)

MA: No that's not true. I miss only one thing in life. Poker.

PHIL: *(Just a hint of excitement.)* You want to play poker?

MA: With *you?!*

PHIL: If you want to—

MA: You are a lousy poker player.

PHIL: I could try—

MA: You're lousy. *(A beat.)* Now *she's* good. *She's* smart. *She* can bluff. I can't bluff anymore. No...finesse. *(Ma points to her throat. She lets out a wheeze. She takes in the cellar for the first time.)* This place is a mess!

PHIL: No one's been down here since Papa left—

MA: He didn't *leave!*

PHIL: *(She's been through this before.)* He's been gone twenty years.

MA: HE WENT FISHING!

PHIL: I know Ma, but he never came back.

MA: Whatever. *(A pause then Ma points at the boom box.)* You're father loved opera and wine and fishing, in that order.

PHIL: I remember.

MA: *(With disgust.)* You got the opera and she got the wine. *(A beat and then urgently.)* Where the hell is she?

PHIL: I don't know. Maybe she got the fishing too.

(Ma makes a strange sound, something between wheezing and choking.)

PHIL: What's the matter?

MA: Oh God—

PHIL: What is it?

MA: Oh God. You almost made me laugh. *(A beat.)* Sometimes you surprise me.

PHIL: Jesus, you scared me.

MA: I can't laugh anymore. It doesn't come out right.

PHIL: You want some diet Coke?

MA: Alright.

(Phil opens a can of diet Coke, pours into two cups, gives one to Ma. They drink. Ma spits out her mouthful.)

MA: This is warm! It tastes like—

PHIL: *(She stands.)* You want me to get some ice.

MA: *(Momentarily disgusted with their routine.)* Naah. Sit down. *(A beat, then gently.)* Sit.

(Phil sits. Ma drinks.)

MA: It's not that bad. I'll pretend it's espresso. *(Ma tries to laugh at her own joke, but can't.)* You see. It just doesn't come out. *(A pause.)* Did I ever tell you about the time your father got drunk and brought home a goat?

PHIL: No.

MA: I never told you that story?

PHIL: I don't think so.

MA: I can't believe I never told you that story. *(A beat.)* One night, your father got drunk and brought home a goat.

(Long pause as Ma stares hard at Phil. Phil waits eagerly; uncomfortably. Finally:)

PHIL: That's it?

MA: What.

PHIL: That's the story?

MA: No.

PHIL: So…?

MA: I was thinking about something else…

PHIL: What?

MA: Never mind. *(A beat.)* So, anyway. One night your father got drunk and brought home a goat. I was asleep upstairs in the bedroom. This was before you were born. In the house on Second Street. In Manasquan. It was right after we got married. In fact, we were just back from Atlantic City. Your father was getting started painting houses. We were very happy. He was very handsome, your father, although a little bow-legged. But that didn't matter. I had the best legs on the whole Jersey shore and we won almost every dance contest at the Asbury Park Casino. There was nothing but love between us. Love love love. That's how it was. *(A beat.)* So anyway. One night he got drunk and brought home a goat. A Billy goat. Don't ask me why. I think it was a present for me. He left it in the kitchen and came up to bed. He woke me up. And that night he spoke to me in perfect Italian. Perfect Italian all night long, because as you know, he came from a good family in Palermo. A *good* family. He couldda been a count if he wanted! He spoke to me in perfect Italian all night. And then in the morning I got up to make breakfast. But there was no goat in the kitchen. Now remember, at this point I still did not *know* he had brought home this goat. So. I put on the water for coffee, and I look at the floor of the kitchen, and what do I see there but all of these little brown…thingies. So I call up to your father and I say: HEY! WHO SPILLED THE ESPRESSO BEANS! And he comes down the stairs with sleep still in his eyes and he says: what? And I say again: WHO SPILLED THE ESPRESSO BEANS? And then from the living room we hear this loud: BAAAAH! And your father starts to laugh and he brings in this goat to the kitchen and he says: THOSE AREN'T ESPRESSO BEANS! And then I started to laugh and we laughed and we laughed…we laughed until we cried— *(Ma tries to laugh, but she can't.)* Don't you get it? It was goat shit!

(Phil smiles and nods.)

MA: IT WAS SHIT!

PHIL: That's very funny…

MA: Well aren't you gonna laugh?

PHIL: *(Tries to make herself laugh.)* That's a really good story Ma!

MA: *(Disappointed.)* Yeah…

PHIL: Yeah…!

MA: Well that's how it was.

PHIL: Yeah…

MA: Love love love…

PHIL: *(A lonely beat.)* I can't believe you never told me that…

MA: Yeah. I can't believe it…and then just a few months later…you.

(Ma and Phil look at each other. Pause. Phil drops her gaze. Ma reaches out and brushes Phil's hair away from her eyes. The wind howls. Upstairs a door slams, breaking the moment.)

MA: Oh my God oh my God, is that her?

PHIL: I don't know—

MA: *(Breaking the sound barrier.)* VIR-GIN-IA!!

PHIL: Ma don't scream—

MA: VIR-GIN-IA!!

VINNIE: *(From off.)* WHAAAT!?

MA: Oh thank God oh thank God.

> *(The door opens. Vinnie stumbles down the steps. She is soaked. She wears a black leather jacket and has a sopping wet blanket draped around her.)*

VINNIE: What the hell are you doing down here?

> *(Vinnie throws the wet blanket to the floor and takes off her jacket. She holds a quart of Jack Daniels. Her nipples poke through her wet tee shirt.)*

MA: Jesus, Mary and Joseph—look at you look at you—

VINNIE: My friggin' transmission fell out on the Garden State Parkway—

MA: How could you do this to us? We were worried sick—where were you?

> *(Ma pops another oyster into her mouth with a mixture of martyrdom and guilt.)*

VINNIE: Nowhere.

MA: WHERE WERE YOU?

VINNIE: I went to Asbury Park.

MA: Are you drunk?

VINNIE: Yeah.

MA: Holy Saint Anthony, look what I got for a daughter—

PHIL: Why did you go all the way out there?

VINNIE: Why do you think?

MA: To see a man, a bum, a drifter!

VINNIE: Yeah I went to see a man!

MA: 'PUTANA'!

VINNIE: That's right Ma I'm a whore, a *tramp.*

PHIL: Stop it—

VINNIE: Oh grow up, Phil.

> *(Phil clutches the boom box and retreats to a corner, she starts 'Vissi d'arte'. It plays through the rest of the scene, which now grows in pitch and intensity. The dialogue is rapid-fire and should overlap organically. Ma swallows oysters at an alarming rate.)*

MA: *(To Phil.)* TURN THAT CRAP OFF! *(To Vinnie.)* You couldda got killed in this storm!

VINNIE: Give me a break Ma—

MA: You couldda!

VINNIE: Well I didn't.

MA: You couldda got killed and then where would we be?

VINNIE: YOU??

MA: Always only thinking about your own self always. SELFISH!

VINNIE: ME SELFISH??

MA: SELFISH!

VINNIE: I work my tits off—

MA: Holy Mother of God—

VINNIE: My tits to the bone so you two can sit around the house getting fat all day long—

MA: *(To Phil.)* Do you hear this? Why is she saying this to me? Why is she saying this to me? TURN THAT CRAP OFF!

VINNIE: Christ, no wonder Papa—Hey, maybe I'll just wait out the storm and then leave, how would that be?

MA: Why is this happening to me?!

PHIL: WILL YOU TWO PLEASE STOP—

MA: I lived for your father! I lived for love!

VINNIE: Oh right!

MA: Love love love!

VINNIE: Then why did he LEAVE!!?

MA: HE WENT FISHING!!!

VINNIE: Oh spare me—

MA: He was a count!

VINNIE: And you were Princess Diana!

PHIL: Stop it—stop it—stop it—

VINNIE: What?

PHIL: Stop picking on her—

VINNIE: Pickin' on *HER?* Oh right, like she was some poor defenseless—

MA: And for YOU what I went through! For my DAUGHTERS. And what do I get in return? I get 'GATSUNGOOL'. NOTHING. THAT'S WHAT I GET!

PHIL: Okay, enough Ma—

MA: Putana!

VINNIE: She's a witch! *(Vinnie pulls up her shirt and flashes her breasts at Ma.)*

MA: PUTANA!

VINNIE: WITCH!

PHIL: STOP IT!

MA: PUTANA!

PHIL: Why didn't you just stay out—

VINNIE: Christ, that's a good question!

MA: PUTAHHHH— *(All at once Ma opens and closes her mouth like a fish gasping for breath. Her eyes bulge.)*

VINNIE: You wanna know why—

PHIL: Yeah!

VINNIE: You wanna know?

PHIL: Yeah!

(The wind is rising outside. Ma is as red as a lobster. She clutches her tin of King Olaf oysters, points at her throat, grabs her neck, flaps her arms.)

VINNIE: No. I mean do you really wanna know?

PHIL: I said yeah—

VINNIE: I came—

PHIL: What?

VINNIE: I came back—

PHIL: WHAT!

VINNIE: I came back to—

(Ma suddenly careens backward in her wheelchair like she was shot from a cannon.)

PHIL: Ma? What's going on? MA!?? MA??

(Just before Ma's impact into the shelves behind her, a hurricane force gust hits the house. The light bulb explodes, the music cuts out. In the blackness we hear Ma's crash; it sounds like a tiny train wreck. We hear boxes tumble. Glass shatters upstairs. Phil screams. Then: only wind, rain, silence and dark.)

"PUTANI COME NOI"

A flashlight snaps on. It illuminates Ma's face. Lights fade up ambiently. Ma stares straight ahead, eyes wide. A large metal tackle box sits in her lap. Phil stands on one side of her. She holds the flashlight. Vinnie stands on the other. She shakes Ma's shoulder.

VINNIE: Ma…? Ma…?

PHIL: Oh my god oh my god…

VINNIE: MA…?

PHIL: Is she alright?

VINNIE: I don't think so… *(Vinnie removes the tackle box. She puts her head to Ma's chest.)*

PHIL: Check her pulse—

(Vinnie holds up Ma's wrist. She puts it down. It falls limply to Ma's side. A trickle of blood flows down Ma's forehead.)

VINNIE: Jesus, Phil…

PHIL: What—

VINNIE: Jesus—I think she's dead.

PHIL: No…

VINNIE: Yeah.

PHIL: No no no…

VINNIE: Yeah.

(They just stand there for what seems like a long, long time. Phil keeps the flashlight trained on Ma's pallid face. Ma's dead eyes shine. Wind.)

VINNIE: Jesus Phil, take that light off her face.

(Phil doesn't move. She is silent, staring into Ma's eyes. Vinnie stumbles to the table, grabs her Jack.)

VINNIE: I need a drink. *(Vinnie sits, drinks, sees candles.)* You got matches for these? Phil? Phil? Phil? Christ— *(Vinnie gets up and grabs the flashlight from Phil, searches the table for matches, can't find any—goes to her jacket, grabs a pack of Newports and a lighter out of her jacket pocket, lights the candles, takes out a cigarette, inspects it, lights it.)* Oh thank god—they're dry.

(Vinnie inhales deeply. Phil finally comes out of her trance and walks down to Vinnie.)

PHIL: What are you doing?

VINNIE: What.

PHIL: *(Points at the cigarette.)* What are you doing?

VINNIE: What?

PHIL: *(Holds her own throat, points at Ma, points at the cigarette, shakes her head.)* How can you do that—how can you do that—

VINNIE: Oh please Phil. Don't start with me. We got bigger fish to fry. *(Vinnie*

gets up, takes candles and places them around the cellar. She sits.) Jeeze, what a night. *(A beat.)* Phil…Sit down. Phil.
(Phil doesn't move.)

VINNIE: Oh brother. *(Vinnie unfolds the other chair and forces Phil into it.)* Sit. Okay. So. What are we gonna do? *(A beat.)* Come on Phil, snap out of it, what are we gonna do?

PHIL: I don't know. *(A beat.)* I think…I think we should cry…I just think that maybe we should cry…

VINNIE: I don't feel like cryin'.

PHIL: I don't either, but—

VINNIE: I was thinkin' more along the lines of callin' 911, you know what I mean?

PHIL: Why?

VINNIE: Because that's what you *do* when somebody dies Phil. You gotta report it, you gotta get them to come down and take away the body, you gotta—

PHIL: Oh no!

VINNIE: What?

PHIL: No Vin, I'm not ready for—

VINNIE: *(Gets up starts up the stairs.)* As a matter of fact, I think that's what we oughtta do. Call 911 right away. You think the phone's workin'? You think it's safe to—

PHIL: No.

VINNIE: No what?

PHIL: I—I don't think it's safe. The radio said we were supposed to stay in the cellar.

VINNIE: *(Listens at the door.)* Oh fuck the radio, Phil. *(Vinnie goes for the door-knob.)*

PHIL: NOOO!

VINNIE: What is your problem?

PHIL: I don't know. I don't want…

VINNIE: WHAT?

PHIL: I'm not ready.

VINNIE: *What* aren't you ready for?

PHIL: *(Haltingly.)* I don't know, I feel like I got something—still to say to her…

VINNIE: Don't you think it's a little bit late for that? I'm callin' 911—

PHIL: *(Stands.)* NO WAIT! I feel like I need to say…

VINNIE: So say it for Crissakes! We're not turning this into a friggin' opera! You got something to say—spit it out and let's get it over with!
   (A pause. Phil is silent.)
VINNIE: God sometimes I swear you're retarded. *(Vinnie exits.)*
PHIL: VIN!
   (While Vinnie is heard on the phone, Phil anxiously circles Ma in the candlelight. She sniffs.)
VINNIE: *(Off.)* IT'S WORKIN'! Hello. Yeah. I need to report a dead person.
   (Phil notices smoked oyster oil dripping down Ma's chin and all over Ma's fingers.)
VINNIE: Yeah I'm sure she's dead. *Yeah* I know her, she's my mother. 27 Maolis Avenue. Long Beach. Yeah. An accident. She choked on an oyster. A tackle box fell on her head. Both. We need someone to come get her.
   (Phil grabs some napkins. She pries the oyster tin from Ma's hand with difficulty.)
VINNIE: Yeah, I'll hold.
   (Phil wipes oil from Ma's hands with the napkins.)
VINNIE: Hello? E.M.S.? Yeah. No. Yeah, she's dead alright. I'm sure you are. Yeah I know. No, she's sitting in a wheelchair. Yeah, it's bad out there? We're in the cellar. Uh-huh. *Tomorrow?!* Uh-huh. Uh-huh. Uh-huh.
   (Phil becomes hypnotized by Ma's eyes. She stares into them deeply and then losing control, she slaps Ma hard across the face.)
VINNIE: Okay. 503-1941. Uh-huh. Yeah, I get it. Okay.
   (Ma's head drops to the side, Phil stands shocked and horrified by what she has done, she gasps, runs up the stairs. Vinnie enters. They run into each other. They scream.)
PHIL: *(Overlap.)* Oh Jesus—
VINNIE: *(Overlap.)* Oh Christ—
PHIL: *(Overlap.)* Oh my god—
VINNIE: Jesus what's wrong with you—
PHIL: Her eyes Vin, her eyes—
   (Vinnie walks past her sister down to Ma.)
VINNIE: What?
PHIL: It's just her eyes…Never mind. *(A beat.)* When are they coming?
VINNIE: They said they'd call first. They got electric wires down on Sycamore, the floodin' sounds bad all over. It feels like the whole house is shakin', and a window bust open upstairs. You can hear stuff blowin' around in—
PHIL: They can't come?
   (Vinnie gets blankets from the table and starts to drape them around Ma's shoulders, careful not to touch her body.)

VINNIE: Not soon.

PHIL: *(Comes down.)* What are you doing?

VINNIE: They said we either gotta keep her warm or lay her out flat or else…

PHIL: What?

VINNIE: Riga-mortis! And I don't exactly feel like layin' her out—So I think— God, she stinks like a big smoked oyster— *(Vinnie gets some candles and lays them around Ma, strategically placing them to create some heat.)*

PHIL: You mean we gotta just stay down here with her staring at us—

VINNIE: You're the one that wanted to have a good-bye talk with her—

PHIL: I changed my mind. Come on Vin, I just can't stand her sitting there staring at us all night long.

VINNIE: Well deal with it.

PHIL: Can't you just do something about her eyes—

VINNIE: No. I'm not touchin' her again, it gives me the creeps—

PHIL: Just close them.

VINNIE: You do it if it bothers you so much.

PHIL: I don't like her lookin' at me!

VINNIE: Then don't look at her.

(Phil paces, takes a white sheet from the table and hastily flaps it out and covers Ma with it. Vinnie sits, her back to Ma, and takes a nice long pull of Jack Daniels.)

VINNIE: Mmmmm. *(Offers the bottle.)* You want some?

PHIL: No.

VINNIE: Come on. Ma's dead…live a little.

PHIL: I said no.

VINNIE: Suit yourself.

(A pause. Vinnie drinks. Lights a Newport. Phil comes down to her. Vinnie keeps her cool through the following exchange.)

PHIL: You know…you are disgusting.

VINNIE: Whoa whoa whoa—where the hell did that come from?

PHIL: Drinking, smoking, what you were doing up there in the bathroom before you went—

VINNIE: What?

PHIL: In the bathroom—

VINNIE: What was I doin'?

PHIL: Before you went out—

VINNIE: What? You were listenin' at the goddamn door? You know what the hell I was doin—?

PHIL: Throwing up your food like that to stay skinny—

VINNIE: *(Laughs.)* Oh you poor fat Catholic thing—

PHIL: Throwing up your food for some man—

VINNIE: Jesus, you don't have a clue—

PHIL: Doing your hair and your nails and then throwing up your dinner for a *boyfriend!*

VINNIE: "BOYFRIEND"!, I mean really—forgive me Sister Philamena Angelina—

PHIL: Well it's true, it's true—

VINNIE: You know maybe if you'd ever gotten laid, Phil, then we could talk—

PHIL: It's Bulimia, it's sick—

VINNIE: But nooooo, not the Virgin of Long Beach—

PHIL: It's a sickness—

VINNIE: *You* are sick!

PHIL: The point is not about me, it's not about me—

VINNIE: *You* are a retarded virgin.

PHIL: *(Works up some tears.)* You are so *bad.* You are so bad—it's not fair!

VINNIE: Poor Phil. Everything's a good thing or a bad thing with you.

PHIL: *(Points to Ma, but won't look at her.)* No, you're just bad. And now look what you've done.

VINNIE: Now wait a minute—

PHIL: You're the one that got her all upset—

VINNIE: Now wait just a goddamn minute here—

PHIL: Why'd you have to bring up Papa, you know how she—

VINNIE: Well it's true, it's true—

PHIL: If you hadn't—

VINNIE: No, you are not layin' this crap on me—

PHIL: And now she's dead!

VINNIE: Excuse me—

PHIL: Because you throw up your goddamn dinner—

VINNIE: Excuse me—

PHIL: And run out on a night like tonight—

VINNIE: Excuse me—

PHIL: To see some stupid "BOYFRIEND"!

VINNIE: Christ, how old are you anyway?

PHIL: No. No. No. Running out on a night like *tonight*—

VINNIE: Because maybe I had somethin' *important* to—

PHIL: NO!

VINNIE: Something' "GROWN UP" that I had to do—

PHIL: No, you are not grown up, you're—self-destructive. You smoke and you drink and you throw up—

VINNIE: Oh would you stop it with that!

PHIL: No. You throw up your dinner!

VINNIE: *(Lightly.)* Because I'm pregnant for chrissakes.

PHIL: *(Still not hearing her.)* No.

VINNIE: Yes. I'm friggin' pregnant.

PHIL: Oh my God. Does Ma know?

VINNIE: Ma's dead Phil.

PHIL: But did she—did you tell—?

VINNIE: What are you nuts? That *really* would have killed her.
    (Phil is silent. Wind. Phil shivers. A long pause. Phil pulls a sweater around herself. Sits. Vinnie and she look at each other. It's an odd moment; charged, ambiguous.)

VINNIE: Christ. I gotta pee. *(Vinnie goes to stairs.)*

PHIL: No Vin, don't leave me alone—

VINNIE: I gotta pee!

PHIL: But don't go up there! You might get hit by a book or something.

VINNIE: Well what am I supposed to do?
    (Phil grabs a plastic cup.)

VINNIE: Oh Jeeze, you gotta be kiddin'!
    (A pause. Phil's eyes plead. Vinnie grabs the cup. Looks around.)

VINNIE: What a night.

PHIL: Does the—does the boy know, Vin?

VINNIE: He does now!

PHIL: And what did he say?

VINNIE: He wants me to have it. *(Vinnie goes behind Ma, squats.)*

PHIL: *(Happy surprise.)* No…!

VINNIE: Yeah. I mean can you believe it? *(A beat.)* Well aren't *you* gonna tell me what a tramp I am?

PHIL: No. *(A beat.)* Who is he?

VINNIE: *(Almost too casually.)* You wouldn't know him. He's just some guy who works the rides at Asbury Park.

PHIL: *(What a coincidence!)* I don't believe it!

VINNIE: What?

PHIL: *(Almost smiling.)* He works at Asbury Park?

VINNIE: Yeah.

PHIL: No kidding?

VINNIE: Yeah! God, Phil, the first time I see him, I'm standin' on line, right?

And I see him. He's loadin' and unloadin' the cars. He's got on blue jeans and his long hair falls in front of his pale eyes. And I mean he is so beautiful, I mean just so friggin' beautiful and unreliable—

PHIL: *(Like a little girl.)* Oh no—

VINNIE: Yeah. Hand me one of those napkins, would you? So, I get to the front of the line and I climb into an empty car of the Cyclone.

PHIL: *(Dead shock.)* The Cyclone?

VINNIE: What?

PHIL: He works the Cyclone—?

VINNIE: Yeah. I told you, he loads up and unloads the cars. So I watch him glide toward me, right and I don't hesitate for a second, but I grab his arm and I say: I like the Cyclone. I like the wet feeling I get from bein' afraid and his eyes kinda—

PHIL: Joey Sclafano.

VINNIE: That's right.

PHIL: Joey Sclafano.

VINNIE: You know him?

PHIL: We went to high school…

VINNIE: *(Casual.)* Oh…

(Vinnie swigs some Jack. Phil is stunned. A moment.)

PHIL: *(To the Jack Daniels bottle.)* Could I have some of that?

VINNIE: Sure.

(Phil drinks, makes a face.)

VINNIE: You want some cola with that—

PHIL: No. *(Phil drinks some more.)*

VINNIE: You alright—?

PHIL: I'm just thirsty.

(Phil drinks again. Vinnie grabs the bottle from her sister.)

VINNIE: Hey! Don't hog it all. *(A beat, Vin drinks.)*

PHIL: You shouldn't be drinking—it's no good for the—

VINNIE: Well I'm not gonna have it!

PHIL: What?

VINNIE: No way—

PHIL: You're not gonna—?

VINNIE: But I have to admit, apart from the throwing up, it does feel kinda excitin'. Like a good sick feelin' in the pit of my stomach—

PHIL: Vin—

VINNIE: Like the time Linda Cavalieri's wig blew off her head when we were drivin' to Deal with the top down, remember?

(Phil turns away.)

VINNIE: Phil…Oh Phil, you're cryin'? Come on, don't cry, don't cry…She had the cancer in her hip and in her throat and—I mean you gotta admit—

PHIL: *(Grabs Vinnie.)* I'm not crying for…I'm not crying for *her.*

VINNIE: *(A beat.)* Oh don't be a silly Philly. You don't have to cry for *me*…I'll be alright. I'll be okay. This is what happens to Jersey Girls. It's what happens…it's almost entirely—predictable. I'll just get rid of it.

PHIL: No! He wants you to—

VINNIE: Well fuck 'em—he *says* it's because I'm the first girl he ever got—

PHIL: Vinnie, you have to—

VINNIE: He *says*… *(Vinnie stops herself. She watches Phil for a reaction.)*

PHIL: *(Blankly.)* Well maybe it's true.

VINNIE: Yeah right.

PHIL: But if he wants you to—

VINNIE: Fuck 'em. Just Fuck 'em—

PHIL: Stop—why do you have to talk like this?!

VINNIE: *(Laughs.)* Because I'm just a slut from down the shore—

PHIL: I don't understand why you talk like—

VINNIE: *(Sharp.)* Because it works for me, alright?

PHIL: Like you have to go out of your way to be—to hurt people—

VINNIE: Why the fuck do you care how I talk anyway—Do you hear me criticize you? Do I ask you why you let yourself get fat like a pig? You used to be pretty, you know. Do I say a thing about the fancy airs you put on, and the fact that you don't do a thing anymore but sit around the fuckin' house like a fungus feedin' on shit?

(A pause.)

PHIL: Do you love him Vin?

VINNIE: Love is a trap.

PHIL: Have the baby.

VINNIE: *(A beat.)* I knew you'd try to lay some sorta "choose life" crap on me—just like Ma wouldda done, no matter what it means to *my* life—

PHIL: No—

VINNIE: And just look at what happened to *her,* what she turned into—No friggin' way—

PHIL: I want to tell you something…

VINNIE: *(So direct.)* So tell me. *(A pause.)* Always above it all, huh Phil? Always our lady of the silences. No. There's no way I'm havin' this—

PHIL: Please Vinnie—

VINNIE: We had plans, goddamit! I've saved up over three thousand bucks.

Payin' the bills, payin' off the car—Still, over three thousand bucks I saved up workin' at Grant's fuckin' sweet shop.

PHIL: *(Softly.)* That's a lot of money.

VINNIE: *(Lights another Newport.)* Damn right. We were supposed to leave for Hawaii. Tomorrow.

PHIL: Tomorrow...? You've been *planning* to leave...

VINNIE: Then he tells me because of the baby he thinks we should stay here, get married—fuck him. I'm leavin' tomorrow with him or without—

PHIL: You can't leave tomorrow.

VINNIE: Watch me. I am not spendin' the rest of my life in friggin' Long Beach New Jersey sellin' salt water taffy.

PHIL: What about Ma?

VINNIE: Oh give me a break! I *paid* my dues.

PHIL: There's the funeral, we gotta make arrangements, and the house and—

VINNIE: Papa was the only one in this family with the right idea—

PHIL: Papa was a coward. He didn't even say good-bye.

VINNIE: Oh and didn't that just break your heart. Daddy's poor little princess...who'll take care of you now?

(A pause.)

PHIL: You think you're so smart.

VINNIE: I am smart. I'm gettin' out of here.

PHIL: You're just running away—

VINNIE: Don't you talk to me about runnin'! I'm *livin'* my life. I've made plans. I've got dreams—You don't have any idea what I'm—

PHIL: Somebody had to stay home and take care of Ma, somebody had to. Somebody had to feel just a little bit sorry for her—

VINNIE: Oh Christ—

PHIL: I can't help it—I just feel so sorry for her.

VINNIE: You are pathetic. You don't *do* anything!

PHIL: I do things, I do things—

VINNIE: What have you *ever* done?

PHIL: I took care of her! What did you do for her?

VINNIE: Oh fuck you! You threw your life away! You threw away everythin'.

PHIL: NO!

VINNIE: Yeah. Even your lousy opera! What ever happened with that?

PHIL: I *know* opera.

VINNIE: What about singin'? What about your friggin' lessons? You loved it and then you threw it away. You quit.

PHIL: I didn't quit.

VINNIE: Oh no?

PHIL: I didn't have the voice—

VINNIE: You didn't have the dream!

PHIL: I just didn't have the voice. Not for Bel Canto.

VINNIE: Oh what the fuck is Bel Canto?

PHIL: It's Italian for—

VINNIE: Christ I know it's Italian. All that crap is in friggin' Italian.

PHIL: It means beautiful singing. That's all. It just means…beautiful singing. I didn't have the voice…Stop. Tell me what happened tonight.

VINNIE: What?

PHIL: Tell me what happened when you told Joey Sclafano—

(A pause.)

VINNIE: What's it to you?

PHIL: *(Urgent.)* Please. Just tell me…

(Long pause.)

VINNIE: (Carefully.) Alright. *(A beat.)* I get in the car. I get on the parkway. I roll down the window of the Camaro and let the wind blow back my hair…

(A moment, Vinnie watches Phil, who begins to wander, sometimes closing her eyes to hear better, after a while Vinnie sits and tells the story for herself.)

VINNIE: I floor the accelerator. I jam on the tape player and pull a swig on my bottle of Jack. "The Boss" sings: "It's a town full of losers and I'm pullin' out of here to win…" I'm thinkin' Jesus, nobody says it like "The Boss." I'm thinkin' Joey will see things my way. *(A beat.)* When I get to the amusement park it's so empty. No music risin' up tinny from the arcade. My black leather jacket is soaked and flappin' in the wind. I head toward The Cyclone. The whole amusement park is spinnin' around me, like I'm the center of a merry-go-round. Little bits of paper swirl around my head like thoughts. I'm afraid I might throw up again. When I get to The Cyclone, I see Joey. He's up on the first slope of the coaster lashin' around a piece of rope.

(Phil stands upstage in the darkness, hanging on every word.)

VINNIE: He sees me and stops workin'. He waves and calls down to me. The wind grabs up his voice and steals it into the sky. I can't hear what he's sayin'—it could be anythin'. This is what I choose it to be: "Will you walk with me out on the wire, 'Cause baby I'm just a scared and lonely rider, But I gotta know how it feels, I want to know if your love is wild, Girl I want to know if love is real." Joey climbs down the white latticed wood of the coaster. He grabs me. His breath is hot, his long wet hair slaps at my face: what are you doin' here, Vin, he says. Joey...I whisper. Baby, we're havin' a storm—or didn't you notice, he says. I laugh and kiss him on the mouth. I tell him the situation and my eyes stare into his. Joey just stands there lookin' at me. The storm is howlin'. The Cyclone is singin' in the wind. Then he tells me that he wants me to have it. That he loves me. That he wants us to stay here! I stand real still. I think my heart has stopped beatin'. A gust of wind comes up from inside me. It lifts me into the air. I float above the amusement park. I am flyin' around in the sky. I feel strange as I zoom above the rides. The Swiss Bob glitters up at me, The Orient Express winks and flashes. I look down at The Tunnel of Love. I feel afraid. The Tunnel of Love begins to suck me down into its gapin' black mouth. I try to fly free of it's pull, but it won't let me go. I'm trapped. I scream as The Tunnel of Love swallows me up into its darkness.

(A pause. Phil comes down, sits. The alcohol hovers over the following.)

PHIL: Does he still drive a motorcycle?

VINNIE: Yeah. A Harley. (A beat.) Listen Phil. It got so quiet. I think the eye of the storm is passin' over us.

PHIL: Yeah... (A pause.) So what happens now?

VINNIE: We wait. He says he needs time to think. That's a laugh. I mean really Phil, he is so dumb. I think I can talk him into goin' but I swear—

PHIL: You know, Vin, you could stay here in the house—

VINNIE: No way—

PHIL: It's ours now, you could stay here.

VINNIE: You're nuts...

PHIL: We used to be so close, you and me.

VINNIE: We were never close.

PHIL: We have so much in common.

VINNIE: You know, it wouldn't be a sin, for once in your life Phil, to tell the truth.

PHIL: That's so unfair—

VINNIE: All you've ever done is keep secrets from me. You and Ma both. Tellin' lies, keepin' secrets. I don't even know who you are.

PHIL: No Vin—

VINNIE: Yeah.

(Long pause.)

PHIL: What will you do in Hawaii? That money won't—

VINNIE: I can take care of myself. If Joey comes with me, he can load and unload…somethin'. That's what he's good at. *(Vinnie begins to move her hands.)*

PHIL: What are you doing?

VINNIE: *(First hint of real drunkeness.)* It's the hula. It's what they dance in Hawaii. They…talk with their hands.

PHIL: You're so drunk.

VINNIE: Come on—dance with me. Dance—let's dance the hula together. *(Vinnie rises and begins to dance the hula.)*

PHIL: Stop

VINNIE: No really. I could finally get to know you Phil. Maybe you'd finally talk to me—tell me your secrets… *(Vinnie keeps dancing.)*

PHIL: Stop! If I told secrets, Vin, it was to protect—

VINNIE: They talk with their hands, Philly.

PHIL: Vin, listen—

VINNIE: They sing with their hands! You don't need a voice—They do—what do you call it—Bel Canto—beautiful singin'! They sing without singin'. Like this—Look! What am I sayin' to you?

PHIL: I don't know—

VINNIE: I'm singin' to you with my hands, what am I sayin'?

PHIL: What…

VINNIE: I'm sayin' sing with me Phil. Sing with me! Sing with me!
(They dance wildly. Phil twirls round and round. Vinnie falls into a chair, laughing. Vinnie claps, smiles. She closes her eyes. Phil twirls: laughing, spinning. After a while she stops, dizzy, sits breathless.)

PHIL: Oh my god—oh my god—Vin? Vin? Vin?
(Vinnie is asleep. Phil gets up, blows out the candles.)

"CASTA DIVA"

Intro to "Casta diva" plays. In the semi-darkness, Phil covers Vinnie with a blanket. She walks around the sheet covered body of Ma. She places bedding on the floor for herself and curls up to sleep. Wind begins to rise again, then falls off. Time passing. Early morning light breaks through the small window. Outside the sound of a Harley revving. A horn. Vinnie wakes up. She hears the Harley, goes to the window, sees something out there and runs up the stairs. Halfway up she freezes. She turns and looks down into the cellar. A moment. Then she quietly walks back down the stairs. She walks slowly past Phil and grabs two fishing poles and the tackle box, then quietly goes to the stairs. A moment. Birds. The cellar is coming alive with colors. More light falls over Phil's body. Vinnie rests the poles on the staircase, turns, goes to Phil, shakes her awake. Light continues to pour into the window. Phil is hung over. She looks around. Intro to "Casta diva" has finished.

PHIL: Huh…?

VINNIE: I didn't want to leave without sayin' goodbye. *(A beat.)* I'm scared. I didn't know how to tell you…

PHIL: Tell me what?

(Vinnie pets her sister for a moment, then quickly goes to the stairs, grabs the fishing poles and climbs to the door. The Harley revs again.)

PHIL: VIN!!?

VINNIE: He told me he used to see you and then one day you just disappeared, and you wouldn't return his calls. *(A beat.)* What happened?

(A long pause.)

PHIL: *(Soft but urgent.)* Do you love him?

VINNIE: Yeah. *(A beat.)* Do you?

(Pause.)

PHIL: Go.

(Vinnie is silent. She exits. The Harley revs in preparation for flight. Phil stumbles to the window. She pounds on the glass.)

PHIL: VINNIE!!

(We hear the Harley speed off into the distance. Phil stands frozen. The phone rings. Phil walks slowly up the stairs, exits, answers the phone.)

PHIL: *(Off.)* Hello. E.M.S. Yes. *(Phil re-enters holding phone. She stares down at Ma.)* Yes. We're ready. Yes. We're ready now…

(Phil drops the phone. She stands staring at Ma. Maria Callas sings "Casta diva." Phil slowly walks down the stairs to Ma. She lifts the sheet slowly from Ma's face, as if she were lifting a veil. She kisses Ma tenderly on the cheek. She stares into Ma's eyes. She closes them gently. She rises and walks forward toward the audience. As the lights fade very slowly, she hulas to "Casta diva." Spotlight on Phil. She is smiling.)

THE END

Slide Show

BY PAUL SELIG

FOR MORGAN JENNESS

THE AUTHOR

Paul Selig's work for the stage has been performed throughout the United States and United Kingdom. Recently, his one-woman show *Mystery School* was produced at The Sundance Film Festival, The Long Wharf Theater, and in New York City at EnGarde Arts; his trilogy of chamber operas, *Three Visitations,* premiered at the Southern Theatre in Minneapolis. *Never Enough* (with Shapiro and Smith Dance Co.) was seen at the Joyce Theatre in Manhattan, and *Slide Show* was included in the Ensemble Studio Theatre's Marathon '96. Other plays include *Terminal Bar; Body Parts; Moon City;* and *The Pompeii Traveling Show,* the recipient of a New York Drama League Award. Selig has performed as a solo artist at the Public Theater, the Ensemble Studio Theatre, and the Circle Repertory Theatre Laboratory. He currently serves on the faculty of the New York University Tisch School of the Arts Dramatic Writing Program and is the Co-Director of the Masters of Fine Arts in Writing Program at Goddard College. Selig is a graduate of the Yale School of Drama.

ORIGINAL PRODUCTION

Slide Show was first produced at The Ensemble Studio Theatre, May 1996. It was directed by Chris Smith with the following cast:

Woman . . . . Paul Selig

CHARACTERS

WOMAN

A woman sits on a chair before a portable projection screen. She is older, elegant, and wears a black dress and pearls. She holds the remote control for a carousel projector in one hand. Her speech is eerily serene. She smiles graciously, her eyes lost, as if in some strange dream.

WOMAN: When Mrs. Hewitt-Packer, having seen last week's paper, called to tell me that she understood I would be canceling this evening's entertainment, I told her no.

When it was first decided to open our home for these public gatherings, I was opposed. There was a guide, then, who walked you through our home with a set of index cards, prepared by me. He would introduce you to the Mayan head in the hallway, and the tribal relics which are encased behind glass in each of our seventeen rooms.

On that first day, I was in the bathroom with the door ajar. And I looked up to see a little Puerto Rican boy staring in at me. In at me and at my left breast, which was protruding from my terry cloth robe like a mute servant girl dumbly accepting her fate at the hands of a new master.

You have taken trains here, or you have walked. You sit beside the esteemed members of the Historical Society whose belief it is that by including you in our salons we might better bridge the cultural differences which have risen up between us. As if by sharing in our collective past we might glimpse our collective future.

You've driven here or been driven here. You have watched for signs along the highway that have led you to our home. You have watched for signs and you have followed them.

You have come for tea and I will offer you tea. You have come for information, and I will offer you information. I have amassed a great deal of information in recent months. My husband's last dig, in Borneo, began in September. I asked him what he was digging for and he told me it was a secret. I doubt, in retrospect, that he actually knew. It is possible that he's been digging so long he's forgotten where he is, so intent is he on finding something that he's halfway through the earth by now. A small man with a spade and a whisk broom, searching for clues to a mystery he can't even name.

I am surrounded by my husband's findings, if not my husband. They inform things for me. They remain constant, reminding me of things. Consuela dusts them, vacuums around them, and around me.

Everybody, that's Consuela in the back. She took your coats, and she will be serving you tea later. Wave, Consuela.

I spend a great deal of time thinking. I have a green chair that I sit in in the study, facing an exhumed statue of a Goddess and a set of spears dating back to the very beginnings of time. I cut out pictures from newspapers when it suits me. I place them side by side on the oriental rug. I compare them.

Mosaics have been created out of less.

I stood beneath one once, with my late godchild, during my husband's excavation on the Isle of Crete. A woman bathing. The tiles collapsed upon our heads as we looked up at her, so enraged was she at being exposed after all these years.

I dream sometimes that I am she. I dream I am in a desert, digging for my husband, who has been buried alive.

Consuela, dim the lights please.

(Slide: an older man in a pith helmet, smiling and shielding his eyes from the sun's glare, which washes out his features.)

WOMAN: This is my husband, on the advent of his last expedition.

My husband is an archeologist. He goes on digs. He violates the earth, reaching deep inside her like an obstetrician forcing delivery. He relieves her of her secrets and marks the sight with great lengths of rope, so that others might see that he has conquered. He arrives home with her treasures, tagged, marked and numbered, which you have come to see.

(Slide.)

WOMAN: An urn, from the soil beyond the Nile River.

Enclosed were a series of parchments, only fragments of which survived their sudden reintroduction to sun and wind.

(Slide.)

WOMAN: Written in Aramaic, they are said to be deviant gospels written at the time of Christ. This particular fragment translates loosely as a list of certain signs or events foretelling an apocalypse, and the return of a deity to the earth's surface.

(Series of slides.)

WOMAN: A petrified fish.

A scarab, in amber.

Bones, fourth century, B.C.E.

My husband has told me that what appears to be the end of one civilization may actually be the very beginnings of another. One has to collect all the evidence to know how deep to dig. Things inform one another. They tell stories. Evidence compiles. From a more recent site:

(Series of slides.)

WOMAN: A child's doll.

A tomahawk.

A woman's shattered skull.

(She has become lost in the images. She snaps back, too brightly, with good humor.)

WOMAN: Would you like tea? I'm not allowed to offer you the good china at these public salons. It is not insured yet and you are not an act of God, which is the only way we'd be able to replace them. If you were, if you were a flood or an earthquake or a tornado railing through the home I would offer you everything, and you might take great pleasure in breaking all of it. All of it.

Consuela?

I read in the Times that there were three hundred more earthquakes this year than last. Most of them were insignificant, of course. Tiny rumblings of the plates, as if the earth were rubbing her thighs together. Then there are the moderate ones, when she opens, anticipating entry. Then there are the ones we read about. When she receives her own and rocks back and forth, crying and releasing, as the shudders continue through her body for quite some time.

Is everybody served?

(Slide: Kali with blood streaming from her mouth.)

WOMAN: The Goddess Kali, Hindu.

Most early objects of religious worship were female.

(Slide: a large figure in maid's uniform faces camera. Shadows obliterate her features. The effect is eerie, foreboding.)

WOMAN: This is Consuela. My husband found her in Equador. There had been a…dig. We bought her a color television set as an incentive for her to live in. She has the room off the pantry, which is just slightly larger than my walk in closet. We put a shelf in there for books. The television set remains in it's carton, the cord still wrapped in it's plastic sheath. The shelf remains empty. What does she do in there alone? What do you do?

(Slide: an excavation of a house in ruins.)

WOMAN: A home from the end of the Roman Empire.

(Slide: a beach house on stilts in flames.)

WOMAN: A home in Malibu Canyon.

(Slide: an elevated funeral pyre.)

WOMAN: A funeral in India.

(Slide: an ordinary rock. She looks at it almost without comprehension, helplessly.)

WOMAN: A…a rock.

(Slide: three children in trance.)

WOMAN: The Fatima Children. Portugal. An apparition of the Virgin is said to have appeared to them in 1917. She appeared before a throng of seventy thousand six months later, as promised. She gave the children dates for the end times. Only one survives, a nun, now, who has taken a vow of silence. She never leaves her cell. What does she do in there all day? A reporter attempted to interview her recently. He wrote that there were circular symbols drawn across her walls, which appeared to him almost as hieroglyphics.

(Slide.)

WOMAN: A Mayan Calendar. It ended some time ago.

(Series of slides: strange circular symbols pressed into fields. She is mesmerized, lingering slowly.)

WOMAN: Crop circles:

> Alabama.
> Surrey, England.
> Indochina.
> The former…Soviet Republic.

(Slide: a huge stone woman, rough hewn, ancient.)

WOMAN: The Goddess.

> I speak very little of my difficulties, except to her. She sits in the study, although she most certainly belongs in a museum. She is one of the oldest objects of worship known to man, pre-dating even the ever-pregnant Willendorf figure by some four thousand years. She's fat bellied and Negroid and her breasts are thick with milk and her mouth a chiseled o, a constant, rock hewn scream. Before she was subjugated by the early church, before she was disguised by the blue veil of a passive Mary, before she was verboten as an object of serious worship, there she was. Waiting. Beneath sand and camel dung in the deserts of darkest Africa.

(She has lost herself completely in this image. She panics, as if trying to retrieve herself from someplace far away.)

WOMAN: Consuela?!

(Slide: Consuela on her hands, washing floor. Light pouring in from a window behind her leaves her in shadow. The effect is serene, almost religious.)

WOMAN: I watch her. I watch her through the French doors of my study as she scrubs the parquet floors, her great arms falling like redwoods into the bucket of soapy water and then slowly across the grain in wide, arched circles. I ask her questions. She doesn't answer…

(*Slide: young man in cap and gown. 1950s.*)

WOMAN: My husband when I met him.

(*Slide: people gathered around an infant at baptismal fount. 1960s.*)

WOMAN: My godchild at his christening.

(*Series of slides.*)

WOMAN: Hurricanes.

Plagues.

Tornadoes.

(*Slide: cave-in at excavation.*)

WOMAN: The Borneo site.

(*She turns away from the image. The slide of Consuela returns. Desperate, pleading, enraged.*)

WOMAN: WHERE DO I PUT THE PAIN?
WHAT IS THE VESSEL THAT CONTAINS IT?!
DO I BURY IT IN THE PARK LIKE A DOG, CLAWING AT THE
EARTH WITH MY FINGERNAILS IN MY CHANEL SUIT?!
FOR IT TO BE EXHUMED AND TAGGED IN TEN THOU-
SAND YEARS WITH THE REST OF ALL THIS?!
WHAT THEN??
WHAT THEN??
WHAT DO I DO WITH IT???
TELL ME, WHAT DO I DO???

(*Slide: ruins, artifacts.*)

WOMAN: Mesopotamia. Gone.

Babylon. Gone.

(*Slide: petrified bodies holding each other, a strangely peaceful image.*)

WOMAN: Pompeii. Gone.

I dream sometimes that I awaken in my green chair and walk past the darkened windows of my home.

Outside, houses float by on new rivers which were formed while I was sleeping. There are winds, great ones, and on them are carried toasters, playpens, cars, and all the relics of a civilization who's time has come.

I see my godson as he was at twelve, carried on a lake of lava. He sits at a grand piano, practicing scales, while around him the white pages of Mozart and Chopin burn like swans.

I look for my husband, and perhaps I realize he is finally gone. That the earth which has reclaimed him is now reclaiming all, for the parquet floor beneath me has begun to shake.

I walk carefully though each of our seventeen rooms. The glass cases are exploding, one at a time, and the bounty that has been preserved within them, Mayan, Aztec, Essene, is finally being returned to its rightful owner.

I reach the kitchen, which has changed. The walls are carved with signs and symbols which I cannot understand, and I crawl into the small, stone chamber off the pantry, seeking sanctuary.

On her narrow bed, Consuela sits, naked and huge. Her stone breasts heaving, sweat beading on her wide, granite brow in anticipation of this, her final return. She smells of the earth from which she has been wrought. I enter her embrace, and I am rocked, and released, and the shudders continue through her body for quite some time after I am silenced.

(Slide: the first one, of her husband shielding his eyes from the glare of the sun.)

WOMAN: You have traveled here. You have driven, or been driven. The Historical Society believes that it is by glimpsing our past we might glimpse our future. There were signs. You have followed them. We have given you tea. Consuela will return your coats now, as you left them. Thank you for coming to our home.

(Looking down and away.)

WOMAN: Goodnight.

THE END

Cats and Dogs

BY CHERIE VOGELSTEIN

AUTHOR'S NOTE

At first, the only person who liked *Cats and Dogs* was my therapist. After a while, my writing group started to come around but still objected to the play's "intrinsic offensiveness," (it was originally set at the Russian Tea Room on "Homeless Night"). Before long, a prospective publisher demanded I remove the "voices." One of the producers insisted I make the "Chinese" waitress German or Swiss. My parents worried how the *New York Times* would respond to the obscenities. The role of Dini went through three cast changes in nine days, I was eight months pregnant, and my babysitter was in a clinical depression. Then the curtain went up. And everybody laughed, especially my therapist.

ORIGINAL PRODUCTION

Cats and Dogs was first produced at The Ensemble Studio Theatre, May 1996. It was directed by Jamie Richards with the following cast:

Michael	Brad Bellamy
Annette	Ann O'Sullivan
Dini	Kate Skinner
Chinese Waitress	Ellen Marinek
Guy	Joseph Lyle Taylor
Person	Thomas McHugh
Voices	Thomas McHugh

CHARACTERS

MICHAEL

ANNETTE

DINI

CHINESE WAITRESS

GUY

PERSON

VOICES

PLACE

A busy Chinese restaurant in Manhattan

TIME

8:10 PM

A crowded Chinese restaurant. Overhead, a sign reads HUNAN EMPIRE, WELCOME TEAMSTERS, LOCAL 247. HAPPY BIRTHDAY VINCENT!

"Voices" belong to various patrons at upstage bar area. Their comments should overlap the characters' dialogue. There is a drunken, dangerous air about the room. A clock reads 8:10.

ANNETTE: *(Toying with her locket, quietly to herself.)* Self-possession, self-possession, self-poss—

MICHAEL: *(Tentatively approaches.)* Excuse me?

ANNETTE: *(Knocking into chair as she rises.)* Oh—sorry—yes—yes?

MICHAEL: You're not Annette, are you?

ANNETTE: *(Hesitant.)* Michael?

MICHAEL: Well! Hello, hello! *(Shaking her hand gratefully.)* Well!

ANNETTE: *(Taken with him.)* Hi! I mean…hi! it's so nice to…

MICHAEL: It certainly is! Ha—have you been waiting long?

ANNETTE: Oh no, not really. Well like forty minutes—but I'm always early for everything—

MICHAEL: *(Checking his watch.)* Ttt, I am so s-s-sorry—

ANNETTE: Oh yeah, no, please, that's fine, really!

MICHAEL: *(Very upset with himself.)* No, it's not fine. It's inexcusable. You see, I never used to be late for ANYTHING. B-b-but my wife, she was always late for everything. So it didn't make sense for me to keep coming early and—and just waiting endlessly so I started coming late too…

ANNETTE: *(Overlapping.)* Oh yeah, no, sure…

MICHAEL: Yeah… *(Sighs sadly, suddenly claps his hands loudly to dispel mood.)* Well! How about if we just…stay right here then? May I? *(He holds chair out for her.)* Kind of unusual place, isn't it? A patient recommended it.

ANNETTE: Oh, yes—

(They sit.)

ANNETTE: —it's just…lovely.

VOICE #1: *(Loud.)* So I says, I says EAT ME!

(Raucous laughter.)

MICHAEL: *(Shrugs apologetically.)* N-n-new York.

(They giggle politely.)

MICHAEL: Okay! so this is okay for you, this seat?

ANNETTE: Oh, yes, it's very—I like it.

MICHAEL: Good, good. You're happy with it. *(Beat.)* I only ask, you see, cause my wife, she would never be satisfied with where—I mean, no sooner would we sit down, she'd be eyeing some spot somewhere else. Very unnerving. So! *(Loudly claps hands again.)* Annette! I have to tell you: I am very, VERY relieved!

(They laugh with relief.)

MICHAEL: I mean I had no idea what Dini was going to come up with, you know? I thought you might be a...a midget or something.

(Beat, they laugh nervously.)

ANNETTE: *(Slightly confused.)* Well I just...when I sit, I guess I look shorter— *(Slaps her face.)* —bug.

MICHAEL: *(Suddenly frightened.)* Oh God! *(Relaxes.)* For a second, I thought that was Dini over there.

ANNETTE: *(Unsure.)* Oh...that would be...awkward, right? Would it?

MICHAEL: Are you joking?

ANNETTE: Oh...you mean because...yeah...it's so true. She just, she makes you feel really comfortable, right?—I mean, here we are, living in the same building, on the same FLOOR for four months not knowing each other and after like what? maybe an hour? I felt like I'd known her 7, 8, 9, 10, 11, 12, 13, 14, 15, 16, 17, 18 months!

(She giggles, Michael looks at her strangely.)

ANNETTE: I was just kidding. You know, by continuing to count. *(She looks down.)* My mother always says...I make jokes no one gets.

MICHAEL: *(Finally gets it.)* Oh I see!

VOICE: The A train, ya shithead!

ANNETTE: *(Plowing on.)* But I really love the building we're in. We have this really great view of Riverside Drive?

MICHAEL: *(Upset at this.)* Yes, I kn-n-n-now. *(Two beats.)* I'm s-s-sorry, I sometimes st-stutter when—

ANNETTE: Oh oh I always get this little tremor in my lip—

MICHAEL: Really? I didn't notice.

ANNETTE: Oh good! Because I'm very self-con—

MICHAEL: *(Looking at her lip.)* Oh okay now I see it.

ANNETTE: *(Covers her mouth.)* Oh!

MICHAEL: No it's cute, it's f-fine...

VOICE: Don't tell me what to do!

(Waitress crosses.)

MICHAEL: *(Upset.)* You were saying...the view—

(FX of dishes crashing, screaming in Chinese as Michael snorts, cranes his neck looking for Dini.)

ANNETTE: *(Covering her mouth.)* Oh, just that I...watch alot of car break-ins.

Like yesterday, I was standing there, looking out the window crying, when this woman got knocked down and kicked right in the stomach on the pavement it was horrible. But I I couldn't move. I just stood there, screaming and screaming with my window closed till the police came. I mean they didn't come obviously because of my screaming, someone else must've called but that's just so typical of me, you know? To do nothing. *(Beat.)* I uh I play the harp—

(FX of cat screech, Annette screams.)

ANNETTE: —Oh my God, a black cat!

MICHAEL: What the hell—!

ANNETTE: Bad luck, that is bad luck!

MICHAEL: What kind of a restaurant is this?

ANNETTE: *(Clutching her locket.)* Oh God, that scared me a little!

MICHAEL: *(Reaches out to her protectively.)* Are you alright?

ANNETTE: Yes, yes, I'm just a little…nervous and… *(Clutching locket.)* — vomity—okay I'm okay having a *very* nice time what a nice tie!

MICHAEL: *(At same time.)* What a lovely l-locket!

ANNETTE: Thank you, I never take it off. It brings me luck—well, it doesn't but— *(Covers lip.)* —I—I'm just a little…superstitious—

MICHAEL: Are you? And yet you live on the thirteenth floor!

(They laugh.)

ANNETTE: *(Puzzled.)* H-how did you know which floor…?

MICHAEL: Oh, well, that's um Dini's floor.

(Waitress crosses, he sucks his teeth, casually asks.)

MICHAEL: So uh…so does Dini have a lot of visitors then?

ANNETTE: *(More perplexed.)* Hmm?

TRUCKER: *(Approaches table.)* Anybody sittin' here?

ANNETTE: *(Starts to rise.)* Oh—

MICHAEL: *(Indignant, pulls her down.)* Wh-what do you think we're doing here?—do you believe?—

(Man walks off.)

MICHAEL: Listen, maybe you'd like to go somewhere else—

ANNETTE: *(Unsettled, covering her lip.)* Oh but I feel like we're, maybe, you know, *destined* to be here or something, I don't know, is that too zodiacky I don't know what I'm saying…

MICHAEL: No, no listen: I don't want to know if Dini has visitors, alright? That is just, that is not something I care to know, okay? You see what I'm saying?

ANNETTE: Oh, uh-huh. *(Uncertainly nods, a bit concerned.)* Do you um do you know Dini well, Michael?

MICHAEL: *(A touch demonic.)* "Well?" *(To himself.)* Can we ever really know a person...but let's see: we met at the end of '86—

ANNETTE: Oh! So for a long time!

MICHAEL: —and then we broke up in March of '87—

ANNETTE: Oh, you went out?

MICHAEL: *(Gives her a funny look, laughs.)* —then we got back together in '88 for six weeks— *(Looks for waitress, waves.)*

ANNETTE: Wow! So you *really* went out!

MICHAEL: —and then we got married in '89.

ANNETTE: *(Stunned.)* What? You...you mean...*you're* the ex-husband?

MICHAEL: Dini didn't mention who I...?

ANNETTE: Sh-she just said, "Michael, the pathologist."

MICHAEL: *(Stifling his rage.)* Yeah, well, that's my little wife for ya, alright! *(Suddenly smashes table with fist.)*

VOICE: Don't bang.

ANNETTE: Oh wow. God.

MICHAEL: *(Worried.)* Alright, look. It's not a problem, is it? I mean—

ANNETTE: *(Hesitating.)* Well—

MICHAEL: —i-i-it shouldn't be—I mean we got married, th-th-that's all—now we're getting divorced, that's it!—l-l-let's have a drink— *(Calls to crossing waitress who ignores him.)* —Waitress—

ANNETTE: *(Stunned beat.)* Getting? Did you, I don't know, did you say "getting"?

MICHAEL: Hmm?

ANNETTE: You mean—you're still—oh God! you're still married?

MICHAEL: Well, in a w-w-w-way but—

ANNETTE: *(Covers her lip, almost to herself.)* Well. Well. A married man. *(Rises, with difficulty.)* Well I'm sorry Michael, but I think this is just...maybe this is not, you know, a good idea after all. *(Beat, hopefully.)* You know?

MICHAEL: *(Pause, deeply depressed.)* I understand. I'll get your coat.

ANNETTE: I...I don't have a coat.

MICHAEL: *(Beat.)* I'll buy you a coat.

ANNETTE: *(Touched.)* I meant, with me. But thank you. *(Standing, hesitates a few beats.)* Oh God, this is hard...I mean I don't really want to go... you're so, so...DECENT but here I am, on my own, alone— *(Slightly hysterical.)* —and and I've decided to take myself seriously for once which is very not easy for me since I'm, you know, worthless and so so I just don't know if it's a good idea for me to be out with the one friend I have's…husband! *(Beat, meekly.)* You know?

MICHAEL: *(Still standing, nods sadly then deeply inhales and exhales.)* The truth is, Annette… maybe it's for the best. I mean, I'm…I'm probably no good to anybody like this anyway.

(They are both very downcast.)

VOICE #1: Hey douchebag!

VOICE #2: Here I am, Harry, over here!

MICHAEL: *(Slowly growing animated.)* But just now…when you were talking about your self-hate—your face, it just transformed into a Christmas tree *(when the tree's plugged in and on.)* —and I think—I think you're…I do. I think you're very, very pretty, Annette—

(She immediately sits, he moves in close, tenderly says.)

MICHAEL: —I love my wife, I love Dini—

(She stands up again, he guides her back into her seat.)

MICHAEL: —I have to tell you that, I mean you don't just stop loving a person the way a…a refrigerator might stop cooling the food if there's a short circuit in the building or a blackout or…or—alright! Dini's damaged. She's very DAMAGED.

(Annette's about to speak, he rolls on.)

MICHAEL: Like a beautiful clock that works enough of the time so you start to think you can depend on it, but then you realize…you realize…

(Cat screech, he's oblivious.)

MICHAEL: What was it? From our first date… *(Getting lost in the memory.)* there she was. On the phone. Screaming obscenities at her mother like I've never heard a girl use before and also, laughing, cocking her head in such a way that I just thought, "She's the one, that's it, she's the one." I mean, she was…never at a loss for words. And so then, neither was I.

(Beat. Annette starts to speak, he continues.)

MICHAEL: With most people, you have to think and think what to say to keep it going, but with her, I never had to think. Not once. It was just so—

VOICE: "Is it a horse's cock?"

(Raucous laughter.)

MICHAEL: *(Oblivious, Annette's about to speak.)* —easy, so seemingly right but now it's over and I won't go into it if that's alright—I was hurt, I admit it, I was *deeply* hurt—because it was devastating, horrible—let's not even dredge it up!—the point is— *(Smiles.)* —instead of feeling dead! I think I feel open to potentially new, very upsetting new pain— *(He reaches across the table for her hand.)* — Annette, what I'm trying to say is: I want to move on with my wife—life—and I think maybe we…I mean, you're so sweet and open, and I…maybe we can help each other—maybe— *(Whispers.)* —do you think it's possible?

(Almost pleading, Annette nods supportively.)

MICHAEL: Do— *(With sudden horror.)* —oh God! Oh God!

ANNETTE: *(Reaches out to him desperately.)* No! I do, I do!

MICHAEL: No, no! It's Dini, it *is* Dini!

ANNETTE: What?!

MICHAEL: *(Anguished.)* She's h-h-h-here—she's here!

ANNETTE: Oh! Oh, you mean like she's in your head even if you—

MICHAEL: No, I mean, she's in the room, she is *HERE.*

ANNETTE: Oh God! *(Starts to turn.)*

MICHAEL: Don't turn around, don't turn around! Do you see her?
   (She tries to nonchalantly turn.)

MICHAEL: You see that bald woman?

ANNETTE: Oh I don't think that's—

MICHAEL: No, no, next to her!

ANNETTE: Wait, she's—oh, oh that is Dini! What a coincidence—oh God— *(Covers her lip.)* —this makes me very nervous I'm going to start talking like a maniac—*(To herself.)* hel-lo!*(Starts to wave almost frantically.)*

MICHAEL: What are you doing?

ANNETTE: Oh—waving.

MICHAEL: No, don't! *(Pulls her arm down.)*

ANNETTE: *(Waving with other arm.)* Oh, you wanted to like pretend not to see her?

MICHAEL: Well, it'd be hard with you waving.

ANNETTE: I'm sorry. My hand just flew up automatically.

MICHAEL: *(Beat, very tenderly.)* You're a fragile, little bird— *(Stone cold.)* —alright here she comes.

ANNETTE: Here she comes.

MICHAEL: O.K. act n-n-normal.

ANNETTE: O.K. *(She knocks salt and pepper shakers over, scrambles to set them right.)* Oh God, that's bad luck—
   (Dini and Guy at table.)

DINI: *(Exuberant.)* Heyyy!

ANNETTE: *(Jumps up.)* Hi, hi, hi!
   (They kiss.)

DINI: I know, I knooooow—this is crazy, right? sick—pretend I'm not here, we are NOT here—I saw you—"Oh my God. Look who it is!"—we had to come over and now we're going. *(Starts off, returning to Annette.)* But can I just say—you look, Annette,—drop. down. dead.—DEAD! Gorgeous! —how do I look?

ANNETTE: Oh, so beautif—

DINI: Oh, I don't care how I look. This is not my night, this is YOUR night. And Michael's night. *(Squeezes Michael's arm.)* And that's why we're going across the room to watch you—kidding, KIDDING. *(To Michael.)* Oh, lighten up.

(She rushes them off as Chinese waitress approaches.)

CHINESE WAITRESS: *(Played by a Caucasian, speaks very loudly.)* You leady to awdaw?

(Michael looks at her sharply, confused by the accent.)

ANNETTE: *(Holds head in hands, dazed smile.)* Oh wow—

MICHAEL: *(To Annette.)* Listen: We are just going to forget she and that troglodyte are here, okay Annette? We can do this—

WAITRESS: You call me over, yes?

MICHAEL: Yes, yes, alright: I'll have…an Absolute—

WAITRESS: If you onry havin' dlinks you haveta sit at da baw.

MICHAEL: Why are you— *(To Annette.)* —why is she talking like that?

ANNETTE: *(Shrugging.)* Well it's a Chinese restaurant.

WAITRESS: Yaw awdaw?

MICHAEL: Alright alright—*(To Annette.)* let's just—are you hungry?

ANNETTE: Are you?

MICHAEL: No, are you?

ANNETTE: Not really, are you?

(Waitress rolls her eyes, hisses.)

MICHAEL: *(To waitress.)* If we don't order food but I pay a little extra, could we just stay here? There seems to be a very strange ambiance—

(Annette holds her head in pain.)

WAITRESS: Amburance? You sick?

MICHAEL: No, no—Jesus! Are you Chinese?

WAITRESS: Do I rook Chinese?

VOICE: *(Person practically leans into Michael's ear.)* Wash your hands!

MICHAEL: *(The last straw.)* Alright, look: do you want to just leave? Maybe we *should* leave.

ANNETTE: *(Upset.)* Oh God, maybe we have to.

MICHAEL: No…NO! I can not allow her to—

WAITRESS: Rook, it vely busy here—

ANNETTE: But this whole thing's so CRAZY!

MICHAEL: I know. Just pretend—

ANNETTE: But just knowing—

WAITRESS: *(Yells.)* ABSORUE AN WHA' ELSE? I GET DE MANAGER.

ANNETTE: *(Overwhelmed.)* Oh God, I'm sorry alright, let me just please have…I'll have a Shirley Temple, okay?

WAITRESS: Shully who?

ANNETTE: Temple. You know, the child star who saved MGM?

WAITRESS: MSG? No MSG.

MICHAEL: No, no—

WAITRESS: Yaw awdaw food—I get de manager—

MICHAEL: Good, get the manager.

ANNETTE: No, I'll just have lo mein, okay? Lo mein.

WAITRESS: Lo mein an wha' else?

MICHAEL: Make mine a double scotch, strong.

WAITRESS: Stwong. An wha' else?

ANNETTE: Um…egg rolls? Do you like egg rolls?

MICHAEL: And egg rolls.

WAITRESS: Egg lolls. How many?

MICHAEL: Two.

WAITRESS: Two. An wha' else?

MICHAEL: Uh…wonton soup. For two.

WAITRESS: Wonton an wha' else?

MICHAEL: Nothing else! Isn't that enough?

WAITRESS: O.K. Two egg loll, wu ro mein, wu wonton soup, wu doubeh scotch, wu Absorue—

MICHAEL: No Absolute. I'm getting the scotch *instead* of the Absolute—

WAITRESS: *(Hisses, turns to Annette.)* No dlink for you?

ANNETTE: Alright, I'll have a Virgin Mary?

WAITRESS: Who?

MICHAEL: Forget it, forget the drink. Just—thank you! God!

(She hisses loudly, exits, he wipes his brow.)

MICHAEL: She's a real wise-ass, that waitress.

ANNETTE: Well, but waitresses have it really hard, always waiting and waiting— *(Holds temples. To herself.)* —I have to relax, I have to relax— *(Dini and Guy are back at table.)*

DINI: Can you believe this? We can not get a Goddamn seat.

MICHAEL: M-m-maybe you should go somewhere else—

DINI: *(Dripping with sarcasm.)* Oh, that's a nice suggestion—

ANNETTE: Why don't you sit with us?!

DINI: Is she not the—you are like…what? caramel! she's a milk dud, you're a milk dud! *(To Michael, about Annette.)* Do I know what I'm doing or what? And you too, Michael, very nice—how's everything going?!

ANNETTE: Oh nothing!—I mean, we were just sitting here, you know—

PERSON: *(Rises at next table.)* We're just about ready to leave—

ANNETTE: *(Covers lip.)* Thank you— *(To Dini.)* —but here, sit here!

DINI: Nooo, I—oh, alright! *(Sits, remembers Guy.)* Oh Guy!— *(Pulls him over.)* —let me introduce you: Guy, this is Michael the pathologist and my new neighbor and best friend Annette. My lover, Guy.
(Guy says "hey", Annette smiles, Michael winces, nods, Guy sits. Awkward silence.)

MICHAEL: *(Quietly to Dini, tries to seem casual.)* W-what are you doing here, Dini?

DINI: Oh. Well. *(Thinks.)* It's Vincent's birthday—

GUY: *(At same time.)* Hey. Fortune cookies.

DINI: *(To Michael.)* I hope you don't think I came here on purpose. *(Beat.)* Do you? *(Beat.)* Well?	GUY: *(To Annette.)* Nice hair.
	ANNETTE: What? Oh!
MICHAEL: It doesn't matter what I think.	GUY: Ya know, you look familiar.
DINI: It matters to me. Well?	ANNETTE: Do I?
MICHAEL: WELL WHAT?	GUY: So how do you all know each other?
DINI: Don't be a baby.	ANNETTE: Well, they're married—

MICHAEL: *(Through clenched teeth.)* Don't tell me what to be—*(Loud.)* I'm on a date here— *(He looks embarrassed as his words fall into the silence.)*

DINI: *(Baby talk, ruffles his hair.)* Oh sweetie— *(To Guy.)* —see, the second I met Annette I fell in love with her for Michael so I immediately set them up and I have to say, you make a really great-looking couple. I have to say that—

ANNETTE: Oh so do you! *(Beat.)* Not "so do you" like *we* do —I mean *I—I* but *you* really do—hel-lo!

DINI: *(Holds Annette's hand.)* No but seriously, don't they just…go together?

GUY: Yeah. They match. *(He winks at Michael.)*

MICHAEL: What do you do. Guy?

GUY: What do I do? I drive a truck—why?

MICHAEL: Well I uh always like to take an interest in who my wife is dating—
 (Laughs boisterously as if this is a great witticism.)

DINI: *(Quickly.)* Guy was a Rhodes Scholar.

MICHAEL: *(Very patronizing.)* Really?

ANNETTE: Oh, you were? That's so impressive.

GUY: Yeah, whatever. *(Touching his nose with his tongue, to Michael.)* Can you do this?

DINI: No. He can't. *(Signals waitress.)*

GUY: *(To Michael.)* You wrestle?
 (Waitress enters.)

DINI: Let's order!
 (Waitress at table.)

DINI: Yes can I—

WAITRESS: Wuh ro mein, two eggloll, wuh woh toh soup fuh two—come later. *(Serving.)* One doubeh Scotch, one Shully Temple.
 (Dini looks at her strangely.)

ANNETTE: Oh, look, you brought the Shirley Temple after all! But you know, I'm thinking maybe I'll get a a little stronger drink—

WAITRESS: *(Shakes her head angrily, hisses.)* Ttt!

GUY: Yeah, and can we get three shots a Daniel's here? *(To Dini.)* You want anything, babe?
 (Michael snorts.)

DINI: *(To Michael.)* What?

MICHAEL: Nothing.

DINI: He calls me babe, alright?

MICHAEL: What did I say? Did I say ANY thing?

WAITRESS: Yaw awdaw?

DINI: You snorted.

MICHAEL: I did not snort! And I don't snort.

DINI: You don't snort? *(To Annette.)* Do you—this man does not know himself—

WAITRESS: *(Loud.)* You awdaw, I get de managah!

GUY: Wait. Are you Chinese?

WAITRESS: *(Out of the side of her mouth.)* Fuck off. *(To Dini, trying to be pleasant.)* Prease awdaw.

DINI: Alright, you have banana ice cream?

WAITRESS: No ice cleam.

DINI: No ice cream? Then I'll take a chicken with broccoli. And coffee.

WAITRESS: Coffee and wha else?

MICHAEL: Nothing else!

GUY: No, no, Annette, you wanted somethin' stronger, right?

MICHAEL: Frozen Daiquiri? Pina colada?

ANNETTE: Or Mezcal, straight up?

MICHAEL: Mezcal? What kind of drink is that?

GUY: Mexican. Very HOT.

(He winks at Annette.)

MICHAEL: Oh are you sure you want that? It sounds kind of strong. *(Waitress hisses off.)*

DINI: What are you, her fucking sponsor? *(Reaches for Annette's hand.)* So you ordered a Shirley Temple! That is so cute!

ANNETTE: Oh yeah, I get that in honor of my mother. See cuz when she was a little— *(To Guy.)* —I was gonna say, "a little girl" but obviously my mother was a girl so I'll just say, "little—"

GUY: Yeah, what the hell.

ANNETTE: —she won a Shirley Temple contest and ever since then, I've ordered Shirley Temples. *(Hits her head.)* "Ever since then." I mean, I wasn't born when she actually won the contest, she was only three when she won but isn't it interesting how cute Shirley Temple was as a little girl and then as she got larger and larger, it sort of just stretched out her charm until there was almost none left—it's funny but do you ever— when you're saying a word—begin to spell it in your head? I was just spelling "won" o-n-e instead of w-o-n—is my is my— *(Laughs nervously.)* —h-head growing?

DINI: Not at all!

ANNETTE: It's just sometimes, I just feel like I have this enormous head or something.

GUY: When?

MICHAEL: I would ask why before when.

GUY: No it's just she's got a big head cuz she's nervous. *(He winks at Michael.)*

MICHAEL: *(Looks at him with disgust.)* She's not nervous! Why would she— she's just making conversation.

DINI: That's right, Michael. Good.

(He glares.)

ANNETTE: Oh it's just my mother is a big issue for me.

DINI: Well Michael was very close with his mother too. She spoiled him to death, you know, acted like she wanted to get down on her knees and blow him every time he walked through the door, right honey? *(Puts arm around Michael.)*

MICHAEL: *(Affectless.)* That doesn't bother me, Dini, if you're trying to bother me, that doesn't bother me.

ANNETTE: My mom spoiled me too, like crazy! I wasn't even allowed to make my own bed—which I wanted to make! She wouldn't let me!

DINI: I like making a bed too! We have so much in common, Annette, it's sick! *(To Michael.)* But I make a great bed, don't I, Michael? Admit it.

MICHAEL: I don't remember, Dini. *(Beat, sinister.)* You tucked the sheets in too tight, alright?

DINI: He's right. I did. I'm sorry. *(Meaningfully, to Annette.)* He's very sweet, my husband—ex husband—whatever he is. I give him a hard time because I love him. *(Massages Michael's leg with her foot. Then grips Annette's hand.)* And I love you. You and him. *(Remembers Guy, stretches for his hand.)* And Guy—

GUY: *(Bashes fortune cookie open.)* Can't get the motherfucker out! *(Reads.)* "YOU HAVE A KIND AND GENTLE NATURE."

(Cat screech.)

GUY: *(He yells.)* Fuckin' cat outta here!

ANNETTE: *(Oblivious, about Guy's fortune.)* Oh how nice—now let's see Dini's—

(Annette opens Dini's cookie.)

ANNETTE: —"YOU BRING HAPPINESS WHEREVER YOU GO."—well!

(Michael snorts.)

ANNETTE: Now mine: *(Reads.)* "SOMETHING TRAUMATIC IS ABOUT TO HAPPEN." Oh God!

DINI: It says that?

ANNETTE: OH GOD!

MICHAEL: *(Consoling.)* No, it's silly, I mean— *(Indicates Dini.)* —"She brings happiness wherever she goes?"—ridiculous! Anyway, it's probably a misprint—

DRUNK MAN: *(To Guy.)* FUCK YOU.

MICHAEL: —they probably meant DRAMATIC—

DRUNK MAN: FUCK YOU!

GUY: Who, me?

MICHAEL: Let's not respond—

ANNETTE: Oh God—

DRUNK MAN: Yeah, what are you lookin' at?

ANNETTE: —these are Teamsters!

GUY: Nothin'. *(Guy rises.)*

MICHAEL: *(To Guy.)* Please don't antagonize him—

DRUNK: You callin' me nothin', asshole?

GUY: You callin' me asshole, nothin'? *(Guy steps forward.)*

ANNETTE: We're gonna get killed!

> *(Annette's, Dini's and Michael's lines should almost overlap.)*

DINI: *(Delighted.)* This is exciting!

MICHAEL: *(Holding Guy's arm, sternly.)* GUY, please!

> *(Drunk walks off muttering, "Ahhh, you're not worth it.)*

GUY: *(Shrugging Michael's arm off. To Michael.)* Hey look. I'm no pussy, alright?

MICHAEL: What's that supposed to mean? *(His beeper goes off.)* I have to get that.

DINI: Don't get it!

MICHAEL: *(To Guy.)* W-what was that supposed to mean? "You're no pussy."

ANNETTE: I have a dog, Kitty?

MICHAEL: Kitty?

ANNETTE: Why? Do you not like dogs?

MICHAEL: No I do. Big dogs especially.

GUY: Ya like 'em big, huh Mike? *(Winks at Michael.)*

MICHAEL: *(Ready to tell him off.)* Listen Guy—

GUY: Wait. *(Beat.)* I gotta take a shit— *(He goes off.)*

MICHAEL: *(Beat.)* He's charming. *(Beeper sounds again.)* Excuse me. *(To Dini, angrily.)* I'll just take this then. One of us is leaving. *(He walks to phone upstage.)*

DINI: Oh please— *(Clutches Annette's hand excitedly.)* Well?

> *(Soft music begins playing in background.)*

ANNETTE: *(Upset, very aware of Michael's presence, covers her lip, whispers.)* Oh Dini!

DINI: *(Surprised, concerned.)* What's wrong?

ANNETTE: I didn't expect...I mean you and Guy—

> *(Waitress arrives with drinks.)*

DINI: Tell me about it. But I had to know what you thought—

> *(Waitress bangs down drinks, loudly, one by one, as they speak.)*

ANNETTE: Of Guy? He's—

DINI: No, not Guy. Who's Guy?

ANNETTE: Who's Guy?

> *(Waitress exits.)*

DINI: I don't know Guy you think I know Guy? I just picked him up at the bar so I could come over—I mean, I couldn't just plop right down like a big asshole by myself, right? But Michael! Tell me! You like him?

> *(A minor scuffle ensues at the bar as they continue, oblivious.)*

ANNETTE: W-w-why didn't you tell me you were married—

DINI: Oh! I forgot—it's insignificant—that's the thing why I need you—

ANNETTE: *(Whispers.)* But I can't get involved with another married man!

DINI: *(Shocked.)* Why?! You're perfect! That's why I picked you!

ANNETTE: But it seems like you two maybe still have feelings for each other and—

DINI: No!

ANNETTE: —you both mean so much to me Dini I just I don't want to get in the way!

DINI: NO, NO, NO! I'm dating Guy now! PLEASE!

(Guy's behind her, puts his hands on her shoulders.)

GUY: Hey. Let's dance.

DINI: *(Dismissively.)* Dance with Annette.

GUY: Let's go— *(He pulls her up.)*

ANNETTE: Oh!

GUY: *(Dragging her onto the floor as Dini primps at the table, Michael still on phone.)* I know you.

ANNETTE: Yes we were just at the table together—

GUY: No I *know* you. From somewhere.

ANNETTE: *(She covers her mouth.)* Well…maybe we were all in a past life together, you know, like where Dini was my brother and Michael was our father and—

GUY: What was I?

ANNETTE: You?

GUY: Was I your lover?

ANNETTE: Oh wow. Maybe you were the gard-en-er—

(Michael turns back to table, continuous. The conversations must intercut without pause.)

MICHAEL: W-w-where'd Annette go? Did she leave?

DINI: It seems she's dancing with Guy.

MICHAEL: With Guy? *(He rises to look.)*

DINI: *(Sarcastic.)* Yeah, is that alright with you?

MICHAEL: Why aren't *you* dancing with Guy?

DINI: Oh just sit down. Guy—

(Annette and Guy are visible, dancing some choreographed steps.)

DINI: *(He sits, she drinks.)* Guy really knows how to move, huh? We go dancing constantly.

MICHAEL: Good for you.

DINI: *(Nostalgic.)* Yeah...remember that move of yours? The spin-around-with-your-ass-out move?

MICHAEL: No.

DINI: *(Drinking.)* Well that's why I'm divorcing you mainly—

MICHAEL: *(Severe.)* Dini, look—

DINI: *(Getting carried away in the memory.)* —dancing around me like Fred Astaire with the coat rack, just using me like some kind of a prop—

MICHAEL: What?!

DINI: —with your hand on my head and that idiotic smile on your face, I'd just want to—unh! *(She grabs him under the table, his eyes bulge in shock and pain as...Guy suddenly kisses Annette. She pulls away.)*

ANNETTE: Guy! What are you doing?!

GUY: Couldn't resist.

ANNETTE: I can't belie—I mean I'm with Michael! I'm Dini's bestfriend!

GUY: Annette, come on, you kissed me back.

ANNETTE: I did not!

GUY: Oh yeah. You did.

ANNETTE: I did n—what are you, the devil or something?

GUY: Just like a little excitement.

ANNETTE: Excitement? You want ex—see this locket? *(She shows him.)* I've got cyanide in this locket. Do you think that's exciting?

GUY: Yeah!

ANNETTE: My-my father gave it to me for my eighteenth birthday—

GUY: No shit! Your father gave you cyanide for—

ANNETTE: The locket! The cyanide I purchased for myself on my twenty-fifth—after yet another cata—

GUY: *(Puts finger on her lips.)* Annette. Annette. *(Beat.)* I *know* you. I could *be* you, alright? *(Beat.)* But I just...drive.

ANNETTE: *(Beat, totally confused.)* What?! *(Serious.)* Look, Guy. Tonight is my last attempt. This is just...the last one—

(The couples' dialogue should intercut like rapid-fire.)

MICHAEL: I like this girl—

ANNETTE: —alright?

DINI: Good.

ANNETTE: So will you please—

MICHAEL: I mean I like this girl!

ANNETTE: —just take me back.

DINI: Good!

(Guy and Annette weave to table.)

MICHAEL: Then why are you— *(Bangs table.)*

VOICE: Don't bang!

MICHAEL: *(Turns.)* Shut up! *(Turns back.)* Why are you doing it, Dini, WHAT DO YOU—

DINI: *(Touches his face, tenderly.)* You, Michael. Michael, my friend, my friend… *(An intense, intimate moment where they almost kiss. Annette taps Michael's shoulder.)*

MICHAEL: *(Leaping up guiltily, knocking things over, very rattled.)* Th-th-there you are! Y-y-you dance beautifully.

GUY: Thanks, Mike.

ANNETTE: *(Covers lip, equally guilty.)* Oh no, were you watching?

DINI: Of course!

ANNETTE: *(Defensively.)* It wasn't me, that was Guy.

GUY: *(Meaningfully to Annette.)* Takes two. *(Winks.)*

MICHAEL: Speaking of which, we're going to go— *(About to lead Annette off.)*

DINI: Wait! Before we split up—a toast. *(Rises, raises glass.)* To friendship— *(Directly to Michael.)* —to everlasting love.
(All but Michael uncomfortably clink glasses.)

ANNETTE: *(Downs drink, gulps for courage.)* Well I…I just have to say one… before we… *(A declaration of faith.)* I believe in signs, omens…cookies— *(In a rush.)* —and and I just know something terrible is about to happen like like we're all about to be…hijacked at any moment. I know it sounds crazy—

DINI: No it doesn't.

ANNETTE: —but I'm afraid! *(Grabs Michael's hand.)*

MICHAEL: *(A bit surprised, makes a decision.)* I'd protect you.

ANNETTE: You would?

GUY: *(Derisively.)* With what?

MICHAEL: *(Deadly.)* With whatever was necessary.

ANNETTE: *(Touches his arm gratefully, touched.)* Oh!

GUY: With your life?

MICHAEL: If necessary.

DINI: *(Calm.)* You would?

ANNETTE: You would? Oh, but don't. *(Holds him tighter.)*

DINI: No, that's sweet. *(Turns to go, turns back.)* You would really die for someone you just met, Michael?

MICHAEL: Yes.

GUY: Would ya die for me?

MICHAEL: No.

DINI: *(Laughingly.)* Would you die for me?

MICHAEL: Would you want me to?

DINI: *(Dead serious.)* If necessary.
     (Increasing tenseness.)

MICHAEL: What's necessary?

DINI: You tell me.

MICHAEL: No, *you* tell *me*.

DINI: *(Fierce and low, deliberate and slow.)* No. You. Tell me.

ANNETTE: *(In a near panic at their private riffs.)* And sometimes I think what if the hijacker said, "I'll kill the three prettiest girls on the plane," and he didn't choose me. How would I feel? *(Clutches locket, begins to grow visibly shaky from this point on. The tension quickly escalates. This is NOT a discussion about dogs.)* I need my dog here I need Kitty. She protects me—

DINI: *(Leaves Annette's side, circles to Michael.)* But Michael will protect you, right Michael? You have so much in common, see, cuz Michael always wanted a dog too, Annette! Only I'd never let him have one. I just couldn't see the appeal, walking behind it, picking up its shit with my little plastic glove, I mean I might as well have stayed married— *(Laughs.)*

MICHAEL: *(Tight, enunciating every word, not looking at her.)* It's called love. Dogs give you love.

DINI: *(Steady gaze.)* Do they.

ANNETTE: *(Staring at her spoon.)* Oh yeah! They give you a love that's unconditional. And that's just such a wonderful thing— *(A tad desperate, to Dini.)* —don't you think it's wonderful, Dini?

MICHAEL: *(Purposefully not looking at Dini, condescending.)* I don't think she understands.

VOICE #1: Squirrels come right up to you—

VOICE #2: No fuckin' respect.

DINI: *(Glares at him.)* Really.

MICHAEL: *(Glares back at her.)* That's right.

ANNETTE: Oh, no, she—

DINI: *(Leaning in close to Michael.)* Then maybe you can explain it to me.

ANNETTE: It's just—

MICHAEL: *(Leaning in close to Dini.)* No. I don't think I can.

ANNETTE: *(Close to tears.)* —just no matter what—no matter how you look—

VOICES: *(Chanting.)* Vin-nie, Vin-nie—

DINI: *(Staring daggers at Michael.)* Are you sure?

MICHAEL: Yes—

ANNETTE: —or how you smell or how much of a stupid failure you are—your dog will love you! *(Clutches Michael's arm.)*

GUY: Sounds like my old girlfriend.

MICHAEL: *(Puts his arm around Annette, to Dini.)* —I'm sure.

ANNETTE: *(Pleading with Dini as she clings desperately to Michael.)* She's always there for you—loving you, licking you—THERE—

GUY: Where?

DINI: *(Tight with anger, turns on Annette.)* Look, Annette. It's crap, alright? *(In the distant background, Arsenio Hall-like "whoo, whoo, whoo" sound.)*

ANNETTE: Wh-what do you mean? I don't— *(Pulling on locket.)*

DINI: *(Very harsh.)* "Love" from a dog.

MICHAEL: *(Protectively interceding, to Dini.)* Let's drop this—

DINI: It's not REAL!

VOICE: Bad decision—

ANNETTE: Dini, that's all I… *(About to break.)* …have here…I—*(Clutches locket.)*

MICHAEL: *(Takes Annette's hand again, cheers from the back for Vincent, furious but quiet.)* She doesn't understand.

DINI: *(Slams table, gets increasingly impassioned.)* I understand. *(Gets up, to Michael, fierce.)* I understand all about "dog love" where ya do what you're told—put the food in the bowl, the dog gives you "love!"—

MICHAEL AND ANNETTE: Right!

DINI: *(To Annette.)* Well WHO NEEDS IT, ALRIGHT?! Love me for my mind, my tits, my CHARM but don't. love. ME.— *(To Michael.)* — because I exist and put food in your fucking bowl that's not what I want— *(In Michael's face.)* —THAT'S NOT WHAT I FUCKING WAAAAANT!

MICHAEL: *(Also rises, explodes.)* SO WHAT DO YOU WANT? *(Beat.)* YOU WANT ME TO WEAR DIAPERS AGAIN? *(Turns to Guy.)* You didn't know she wanted me to wear diapers, did you, Guy?

GUY: No, she never mentioned—

DINI: Michael, shut up!

MICHAEL: Well, it's true—so I wouldn't l-l-leave. HAH!

ANNETTE: Leave?

MICHAEL: You know, to go to the bathroom, leave her side—

DINI: I'd think you'd appreciate—

ANNETTE: I can see how— *(Takes locket off.)*

DINI: Anyway, IT WAS A JOKE!

(Annette opens locket.)

GUY: I don't get it.

MICHAEL: Yeah, me either.

DINI: That's right you don't you never did—

MICHAEL: That's right! I didn't, I don't!

DINI: *(Close to crying.)* Because I wanted you there for me—you fucker!

ANNETTE: Ohhhh God— *(Takes cyanide out.)*

MICHAEL: *(Also close to crying.)* I was there, Dini, *I* was there. YOU'RE the one who left—

VOICE: You gotta get call waiting!

MICHAEL: *(Desperate.)* I did everything, I tried everything—

DINI: Oh right! You and your fucking dog bullshit sitting there—be a little honest for once in your—unconditional love my fucking fucking ass sitting there holding— *(Crying.)* —Annette's Goddamn fucking hand right in front of me!

(He pulls his hand away.)

ANNETTE: Oh no oh no— *(Pours cyanide into water glass.)*

MICHAEL: Oh Jesus—

DINI: RIGHT IN FRONT OF ME—

MICHAEL: *(Horrified.)* Not another test? Not another test?

DINI: —MICHAEL!

MICHAEL: *(Completely blown away, pleading for his life.)* But I thought we were finished—I failed, didn't I?! I failed!!

(Annette holds glass up with shaking hands as Michael begins pacing like a caged animal, pulls at his hair, appeals to the others, about Dini.)

MICHAEL: What can I do? Tell me what can I do? What can I do to please this crazy Goddamn bottomless pit just TELL ME AND I'LL DO IT— *(At her knees.)* — DINIIIII!

(They are silent a long time.)

ANNETTE: *(Inhales deeply.)* Yeah well— *(Holds glass to her mouth. Starts to shake violently as the eruption begins.)* —I am here, I am...HERE— *(Starts throwing things off table.)* —and you can't just KISS me KISS ME YOU GUY just because you feel like it I am not a fork or or castenettes—I matter Dini Michael a marriage, children, friendship— ME— *(Begins to psychotically rant.)* —IT WAS A BAD DECISION THEY COME RIGHT UP TO YOU INFORMATION HIGHWAY NO RESPECT TAKE THE A TRAIN WASH YOUR HANDS HORSE'S COCK DON'T TELL ME WHAT TO DO DOUCHE BAG DOUCHE BAG HE CONTINUES JUST ADMIT IT BAD DECISION TELL ME WHY WHY WHY WHY WHY WHY— *(Soft.)* —can't *I* be *the one*— *(To people at next table, screams.)*

—YOU SAID YOU WERE LEAVING! *(Frenzied conversation with her-self.)* But I mean, who am I kidding, who am I kidding, he still loves her, they're still married, I don't even know him but I just stay, waiting and waiting, because something's missing, some part some *thing* some PART that makes people walk AROUND you instead of OVER you I don't have because I'm nothing, I'm background, I'm white noise— *(Points to clock.)* —it's TOO LATE!—ME—city, me, streets, me, rooms, me, everywhere—none of us—all of us—got it—ME—the milk—the milk— enough—please—let me be a dog— *(Throatbreaking scream.)* — PLEEEEASE! I DESERVE A FUCKING NIGHT!

(She throws glass across the room. They all stand in stunned, terrified silence, Guy looking at Annette, Dini and Michael behind him looking at floor.)

PERSON: *(Passing by, to Annette.)* Anybody sittin' here?

ANNETTE: Yes. *(Sits.)* I'M sitting here. *(Beat.)* This is *my* table. *(Beat.)* Here. I. Am.

(The lights slowly fade to black.)

THE END